ENCOUNTERS

WITH

JESUS

ENCOUNTERS

WITH

JESUS

*Forty Reflections on Knowing
and Loving the Savior*

J.R. HUDBERG

Our Daily Bread
Publishing™

*Encounters with Jesus: Forty Reflections on Knowing
and Loving the Savior*
© 2022 by J.R. Hudberg

Interior design by Michael J. Williams

Library of Congress Cataloging-in-Publication Data

Names: Hudberg, J.R., author.
Title: Encounters with Jesus : forty reflections on knowing and
    loving the Savior / J.R. Hudberg.
Description: Grand Rapids, MI : Our Daily Bread Publishing,
    [2022] | Summary: "Encounters with Jesus: Forty Reflections
    on Knowing and Loving the Savior encourages you to accept
    the risk and follow Christ"--Provided by publisher.
Identifiers: LCCN 2021039288 | ISBN 9781640701397
Subjects: LCSH: Jesus Christ--Friends and associates--Miscella-
    nea. | Bible stories, English--New Testament. | Bible. Gospels-
    -Miscellanea. | God (Christianity)--Worship and love--Mis-
    cellanea. | BISAC: RELIGION / Christian Living / Spiritual
    Growth | RELIGION / Christian Living / Inspirational
Classification: LCC BS2430 .H83 2022 | DDC 231--dc23
LC record available at https://lccn.loc.gov/2021039288

Printed in the United States of America
22 23 24 25 26 27 28 29 / 8 7 6 5 4 3 2

CONTENTS

Introduction: Before You Begin This Forty-Day Journey

1. The Sentimental, *Luke 2:16–20*
2. The Faithful, *Luke 2:25–35*
3. The Hurt, *Luke 2:41–50*
4. The Unwanted, *John 4:15–42*
5. The Obedient, *Luke 5:1–11*
6. The Hopeful, *Matthew 8:1–4*
7. The Seeker, *Mark 2:1–12*
8. The Offended, *Matthew 9:9–13*
9. The Broken, *John 5:1–14*
10. The Self-Righteous, *Mark 3:1–6*
11. The Uninitiated, *Matthew 8:5–13*
12. The Vulnerable, *Luke 7:11–17*
13. The Confused, *Matthew 11:1–6*
14. The Dismissive, *Luke 7:36–50*
15. The Perplexed, *Matthew 13:10–23*

16. The Rescued, *Mark 4:35–41*
17. The Grateful, *Mark 5:14–20*
18. The Bold, *Mark 5:24–34*
19. The Heartbroken, *Mark 5:35–43*
20. The Skeptical, *Mark 6:1–6*
21. The Willing, *Mark 6:31–44*
22. The Courageous, *Matthew 14:22–33*
23. The Hard-Hearted, *Mark 6:45–52*
24. The Despairing, *Mark 7:24–30*
25. The Inspired, *Matthew 16:13–20*
26. The Desperate, *Mark 9:14–27*
27. The Condemned, *John 8:2–11*
28. The Confident, *Luke 10:25–37*
29. The Distracted, *Luke 10:38–42*
30. The Fixated, *John 11:17–37*
31. The Antagonistic, *John 11:45–50; Mark 14:55–64*
32. The Exiled, *Luke 17:11–19*
33. The Zealous, *Luke 22:47–51*
34. The Faithless, *Luke 22:54–62*
35. The Curious, *John 18:33–38*
36. The Convert, *Luke 23:32–43*
37. The Surprised, *Luke 24:13–35*
38. The Disillusioned, *John 21:2–7*
39. The Remorseful, *John 21:15–19*
40. The Witnesses, *Matthew 28:16–20; Acts 1:6–9*

BEFORE YOU BEGIN THIS FORTY-DAY JOURNEY

Many of us have wondered what it would have been like to encounter Jesus face-to-face, to have His words travel directly from His lips to our ears or see His divine power restore blind eyes, calm the stormy sea, or turn a snack into a feast. How would you have reacted? What would it have been like to experience Jesus's presence and power during His earthly ministry?

What would it have felt like to have been standing beside the widow who was grieving the death of her son when Jesus looked at her and said,

"Don't cry"? Or imagine being there with Mary and Martha when Jesus *didn't* show up to heal their brother. What about the paralytic whose sins were forgiven before his legs were healed? What would you have thought in that moment?

For the next forty days, we'll explore together, through some creative retelling, what some of those who saw and heard Jesus may have experienced. You'll first read the story as it is told in Scripture, then taking cues from the biblical account and using a bit of imagination, you'll step into the story again as someone may have experienced it, exploring the thoughts and emotions people may have grappled with as they witnessed the surprising work of Jesus.

At times, the Bible gives us hints about what people were thinking and feeling, but it doesn't often give us the details we might like. My hope is that by using some "holy imagination" we can find ourselves in these stories in a new way and, like the characters in them, walk away changed by an encounter with Jesus.

THE SENTIMENTAL

Luke 2:16–20

So they hurried off and found Mary and Joseph, and the baby, who was lying in the manger. When they had seen him, they spread the word concerning what had been told them about this child, and all who heard it were amazed at what the shepherds said to them. But Mary treasured up all these things and pondered them in her heart. The shepherds returned, glorifying and praising God for all the things they had heard and seen, which were just as they had been told.

Mary sat and pondered, not just the events of the night, but everything that had led to that moment.

The shepherd's story forced her back to the night Gabriel appeared.

Gabriel. Mary may have wondered if he was the one the shepherds saw. Miraculous births seemed to be part of his mission. Zechariah said that Gabriel told him about the coming pregnancy of Elizabeth. He may have been the one who visited Joseph in a dream too. Angels had delivered some astonishing messages about this little child.

Mary remembered Gabriel's visit. As scared as the shepherds had said they were when the angel showed up in the sky overhead, that wasn't what Mary remembered. The disturbing part of Gabriel's arrival wasn't the sudden appearance of the heavenly figure; it was what he said: "Greetings, you who are highly favored! The Lord is with you" (Luke 1:28). What did that mean? He didn't explain. Not really. He only said she had found favor with the Lord. Why? What for?

Mary thought of Gabriel's words. She had become pregnant despite being a virgin. She cradled the boy in her arms and smiled at him. She still wasn't entirely sure why she had been chosen for this joy. Gabriel had said she was favored.

He even repeated it. As the infant grabbed her finger, she knew she was indeed favored.

Mary looked at her son. How would He become king? This little one was to sit on David's throne forever, but she was a simple girl, and Joseph a carpenter. How would their child become the ruler of Israel? Surely the God who gave her the child could give the child the throne, but Mary wondered, How? When? What would it mean for her and Joseph? How would they raise a King?

As she gazed at the infant King, Mary thought again of the angel's message to Joseph. She remembered him telling her about his dream and why the angelic visit had been necessary. Joseph believed she had been unfaithful and confessed he had planned to divorce her. She had tried to explain. She had told Joseph about Gabriel's visit, of her faithfulness to him and the divine source of the life in her womb. She understood how implausible the whole thing must have seemed; she was still grappling with the reality herself. It wasn't surprising that a heavenly message was needed to convince him.

She remembered the change in Joseph after

his dream. She recalled his words of love and commitment to her and her unborn child, the boy who would be "God with us." She knew this would be a difficult path for both of them.

Mary reflected on what the angel had told Joseph of the child's destiny: "He will save his people from their sins."

None of this had been a part of her girlhood fantasies. Good Jewish girls don't find themselves pregnant before marriage. She had wondered what her family would say. She knew if Joseph didn't believe her, they had no reason to. She remembered not knowing how she would face her friends or go to synagogue. Most of all, she remembered feeling she was in over her head.

As she sat with the animals, she remembered the glances and whispers. She had guessed what they said about her and about Joseph, and she had feared what they would say about her child. But looking down at her son, the fact that, in her innocence, she had endured the accusations of sin, mattered little. The bundle in her arms was going to save people from their sins.

Mary remembered these events, and she

pondered the future of the baby in her arms: ruler, Savior, God with us.

She didn't know what it would mean to raise this little one. She wondered whether the advice given to other mothers would apply to raising "God with us." Mary had already been filled with emotion, thinking back on all that had led her to this beautiful moment—and that was before the shepherds had entered.

Mary had smiled as their timid heads peeked around the corner, respectful but obviously excited.

Awkward introductions had followed. Strangers wanted to see her baby, her Jesus. Didn't they know how special He was? They did. Mary listened as they recounted their tale. Another angel with another message from heaven about her son. Mary's growing wonder—planted by the angelic message given to her, nurtured by the angel's words to Joseph, and fostered further by her cousin's beautiful words about her unborn baby—were confirmed to the shepherds. And not by just one angel, but an entire host.

Mary watched these strangers stare at her son as she thought of that single word the shepherds had repeated: *Messiah*. Jesus, her new baby, the child who, not many hours ago, was still in her womb, was King, Savior, Messiah. How could she raise Messiah? What would she tell Him? What would she *need* to tell Him? A new mother has so much to learn, but to raise the Messiah? Her mind continued to ponder all the things the prophets had said about the coming of the Promised One.

There was much to treasure and ponder.

REFLECT

It's easy to be infected by the shepherds' excitement and wonder. But perhaps Mary is our example. Has it has been a while since you contemplated the meaning and depth of the birth of Jesus, our King and Savior? Where do you live in allegiance to this King and His kingdom? Are there places in your heart still in rebellion? Why?

Jesus, thank You for giving up Your glory in the presence of the Father and coming to join us and experience life as one of us. Thank You for the redemption Your life, death, and resurrection made possible. Sometimes it is easy to take for granted the things we know about You and what You have done.

I confess that I do not always spend time pondering everything Your coming meant and means. Help me to take time to reflect on who You are and what it means to be part of Your kingdom. Amen.

2

THE
FAITHFUL

Luke 2:25–35

Now there was a man in Jerusalem called Simeon, who was righteous and devout. He was waiting for the consolation of Israel, and the Holy Spirit was on him. It had been revealed to him by the Holy Spirit that he would not die before he had seen the Lord's Messiah. Moved by the Spirit, he went into the temple courts. When the parents brought in the child Jesus to do for him what the custom of the Law required, Simeon took him in his arms and praised God, saying:

> "Sovereign Lord, as you have promised,
>   you may now dismiss your servant
>   in peace.
> For my eyes have seen your salvation,
>   which you have prepared in the sight

of all nations:
a light for revelation to the Gentiles,
and the glory of your people Israel."

The child's father and mother marveled at what was said about him. Then Simeon blessed them and said to Mary, his mother: "This child is destined to cause the falling and rising of many in Israel, and to be a sign that will be spoken against, so that the thoughts of many hearts will be revealed. And a sword will pierce your own soul too."

Simeon sat in the outer court of the temple, watching, waiting, his eyes flitting eagerly over the people coming to offer their sacrifices.

Today had to be the day. The Spirit had urged him to the temple. He knew it was the Spirit. He had felt the Spirit before, and the feeling was unmistakable. God had made him a promise, and it was about to be fulfilled.

He would see, with his own eyes, the Lord's Messiah—the Anointed One who would restore Israel and fulfill the promises God made to His people, the one who would bring peace and prosperity, forgiveness and restoration. Simeon would see Him before he died.

In the early days, he was sure the promise was imminent; everyone was a possible Messiah. Simeon watched, examined, speculated. The knowledge that death lay on the other side of the promise fulfilled was a distant dark cloud bathed in the light of Messiah's coming. It held no threat in comparison to the joy of the promise.

He had learned patience as he waited for his promise. The lesson that Israel had been learning about God's timing became his as the days turned to weeks and the weeks to years. The strength of his youth made room for the wisdom of his age.

His eyes would see the salvation promised by God so long ago. The years Israel had waited for Messiah were coming to an end, and Simeon's own waiting would mark the final days of Israel's long patience.

Years passed, but that had not dulled his anticipation. Simeon still watched and waited, much as he was doing now. People came and went as they always had. Simeon watched, as he always had. How many times had he sat here waiting to see the Promised One? He sat in "his place" in the temple courts, watching, waiting, and studying. His time spent reading had given him a deeper understanding of who Messiah would be and what He would do.

Simeon reflected on the day he told Anna of his promise. Astonishment and joy mingled into an expression Simeon would never forget. Since then, the two had often talked, always about the coming of the Messiah.

They discussed the one who would bring comfort to Israel, who would soothe the wounded identity brought on by years of subjugation to Gentile rulers. Messiah would bring comfort through the presence of God. Messiah, Anna and Simeon agreed, would bring true glory back to Israel; God would once again dwell with His people.

They wondered together that Israel would be a light to the Gentiles. Soon, people from every nation would stream into Israel to learn of God and be taught His ways. Israel would stand as a beacon of hope and peace, summoning all people to hear the words of the Lord.

Simeon remembered these conversations as he sat in the temple. He remembered the promises of God, and he contemplated the coming kingdom.

He scanned the faces of the men who walked past, each one a possibility. But as each passed, the Spirit was silent.

Then came a couple to dedicate a newborn—tiny, barely a month old. It was a poor couple. Simeon could see the doves they brought to offer. Why had his heart caught? Was this man with a small child the one? He looked again. But the Spirit drew his eyes to the child.

Simeon moved, the stiffness of his old bones forgotten as he approached the couple with the infant. So small, and yet this was Him. This was Messiah. The Spirit was clear.

He chuckled to himself as he drew closer. Years of looking for the one who would take the throne had led him to expect something different—certainly not a baby. Yet here in this babe rested the fulfillment of Israel's hopes. Certainly, the chosen one would have to have been an infant at some point, but Simeon had expected that he would see Messiah as the one ready to usher in the promises, not as the newborn who would grow into that man.

It didn't matter. God's promise to Simeon was true, and it was now fulfilled.

He approached the couple with wonder in his eyes. His request to hold the baby was met with polite but curious and cautious permission. *Jesus.* His name was Jesus. Simeon understood the meaning.

REFLECT

The unexpected appearance of an infant as the one who would fulfill the promises God had made over the centuries reminded Simeon that God's ways are not human ways. Our expectations may lead us to look for the wrong things. Are there things you are expecting from God? Are you open to the truth that God does not often work in ways that make the most sense to us? How might your ideas of God and your expectations become a barrier to your relationship with Him?

God of Surprises, Your story of redemption shows You are a God who does the unexpected in unexpected ways. You use the unlikely to tell Your story, and You are continuing to tell it, with and through us. Thank You for allowing us to be a part of it.

I confess that sometimes I think I know what the next scene should be. My expectations threaten to change the script from Your story to mine. Forgive me for the times when I thought I knew precisely what You were doing. Forgive me for not following the leading of Your Spirit. Help me to recognize when my expectations are coloring my understanding. Help me to play my part in Your redemption story. Amen.

THE
HURT

Luke 2:41–50

Every year Jesus' parents went to Jerusalem for the Festival of the Passover. When he was twelve years old, they went up to the festival, according to the custom. After the festival was over, while his parents were returning home, the boy Jesus stayed behind in Jerusalem, but they were unaware of it. Thinking he was in their company, they traveled on for a day. Then they began looking for him among their relatives and friends. When they did not find him, they went back to Jerusalem to look for him. After three days they found him in the temple courts, sitting among the teachers, listening to them and asking them questions. Everyone who heard him was amazed at his understanding and his answers. When his parents saw him, they were astonished. His mother said to him, "Son, why have you treated us like this? Your father and I have been anxiously searching for you."

"Why were you searching for me?" he asked. "Didn't you know I had to be in my Father's house?" But they did not understand what he was saying to them.

The excitement of Passover had invigorated the travelers. Weak and tired limbs were easily forgotten as the streets teemed with friends, family, ceremony, and celebration. For seven days, they had remembered God's deliverance. They had told and retold the story. They recalled God's power in the plagues of Egypt, recounted Moses's speeches before Pharoah, and partaken in a meal to commemorate the night God spared their ancestors through the mark of lamb's blood on their doors. Along the way, they told their own stories of God's faithfulness, power, and presence in their lives.

Of course, memory is fickle, and the annual rehearsal was a high point that would recede. Life would go on. But for now, on the first day of the journey home, the excitement in the large group of travelers was still palpable. And so, they walked, and they spoke, and they thought everyone was accounted for.

The day drew late, and the large group stopped for the evening. As the initial chaos of camp settled into pockets of fires and tents, the smell of roasting food began to waft through the air. Called out names joined the smells permeating the air. Parents welcomed their children for the night. Raucous talk and laughter dulled into the low murmur of close conversation.

All but one campsite had settled. All but one was quietly enjoying the calm evening. Mary and Joseph were still setting up camp, busy with the preparations of the tent and the meal. But Mary was distracted, her motions tense. Frequently she straightened from her task. "Jesus!" she called more than once, but silence was the only reply she received.

This was not Jesus's first Passover journey with His parents. He knew the routine and should have found them. He should have responded to His mother's calls. Jesus knew, even in the excitement of travel, there were jobs to do, responsibilities to attend to.

Mary made her way to the other tents and fires. The thought that He was not with the company had not entered her mind. After each tent with no Jesus, she was certain He would be in the next. She moved from family tents to those of friends. Still, there was no Jesus. "We haven't seen Him all day," was the common refrain in tent after tent, and it was enough to plant the first seeds of real worry in her mind.

The worry pushed her to move faster and faster. She was desperate to find her son, and she could barely contain the fear that scratched at her heart. Others had joined in the search. First Joseph, then family, and eventually most of the caravan was calling for Jesus. But the shouts of His name were only answered by more shouts. Soon, the whole camp had been searched. Jesus had not been found, and Mary realized He had not been seen since Jerusalem.

Jerusalem. They had to go back. Mary would not wait until morning. Joseph asked family to look after their tent and possessions, and the nervous parents set out for Jerusalem. Sleep would have eluded them that night anyway, and travel offered both a distraction and the consolation of knowing they were doing something to find their missing son.

In Jerusalem, steps were retraced, acquaintances visited, descriptions given, questions asked, but there was no sign of Jesus. After three days of searching, Mary and Joseph were exhausted and distraught, by turns scared, frustrated, angry, depressed, confused. The disappearance of their son had depleted them of everything.

Where was He sleeping? What was He eating? What had He been doing? Was He okay?

The temple seemed to be the last place left to look. They stood, scanning the people. When Mary's eyes landed on a cluster of people, her hand instinctively reached for Joseph's. There, sitting among the teachers of the law was a young boy. She was not sure it was Jesus until she heard Him speak. He was asking, and answering, questions. Everyone was astonished at His wisdom. Her relief brought tears, but they were not tears only of joy and relief; they were tears of pride as well.

But the moment was too long, and Mary burst into the crowd. "Son, why have you treated us like this? Your father and I have been anxiously searching for you."

Jesus's response was as simple as it was confusing, "Why were you searching for me?" He asked. "Didn't you know I had to be in my Father's house?" Every parent knows the simple answer to the first question. But Jesus's meaning (and the confusing part of His reply) was couched in the second. There was no need to search, because they should have known where He would be.

REFLECT

Life moves at a hectic pace, and day-to-day activities can become so routine that we simply expect things to stay the same. What if you stopped to find "Jesus is not with you," that you had gone ahead without Him? How would you respond? Jesus is always going about His Father's work—and it's our job to follow Him, not the other way around. When it's time to find Jesus, where and how will you look for Him?

Savior, as we follow You, help us to remember
You are concerned with Your Father's business,

*and so, too, should we be. In the pace of every-
day life, we can forget to "check and see" that
You are with us.*

*Forgive me for the times when I have taken
Your presence for granted. Thank You that Your
invitation to follow You is always open to me.
Give me the strength and courage to journey
with You wherever You lead. Amen.*

4

THE UNWANTED

John 4:15–20, 25–26, 28–30, 39–42

The woman said to him, "Sir, give me this water so that I won't get thirsty and have to keep coming here to draw water."

He told her, "Go, call your husband and come back."

"I have no husband," she replied.

Jesus said to her, "You are right when you say you have no husband. The fact is, you have had five husbands, and the man you now have is not your husband. What you have just said is quite true."

"Sir," the woman said, "I can see that you are a prophet. Our ancestors worshiped on this mountain, but you Jews claim that the place where we must worship is in Jerusalem."

The woman said, "I know that Messiah" (called Christ) "is coming. When he comes, he will explain everything to us."

Then Jesus declared, "I, the one speaking to you—I am he."

Then, leaving her water jar, the woman went back to the town and said to the people, "Come, see a man who told me everything I ever did. Could this be the Messiah?" They came out of the town and made their way toward him.

Many of the Samaritans from that town believed in him because of the woman's testimony, "He told me everything I ever did." So when the Samaritans came to him, they urged him to stay with them, and he stayed two days. And because of his words many more became believers.

They said to the woman, "We no longer believe just because of what you said; now we have heard for ourselves, and we know that this man really is the Savior of the world."

The sun at its peak made the heat nearly unbearable. Not the ideal time for manual labor. But the early morning hours for drawing water were not an inviting time for everyone, at least not for her. It hadn't taken many mornings for her to decide that suffering the heat and sun was preferable to the scorn and ridicule of her neighbors.

The solitude, however peaceful, was a painful reminder of how difficult her life had been. *Were they right about her value? Her character? Was she less than the rest of them?*

She didn't need them; she had her man. But even that thought was dampened by a nagging question that rose in her mind—*for how long?* They were correct; he was not her first, not even her second, nor her . . . She didn't *need* the townspeople, but she wanted them. She longed to be part of the community, to know the joy and security of acceptance and a relationship that lasted.

Today would be no different. With a jar on her shoulder she left her home. She looked around as she made her way to the well. The side stares were normal. She still noticed them, but routine has its benefits, and she no longer cried.

She stopped when she saw the figure sitting at the well. A moment's indecision held her. With a sigh, she steeled herself. A man at the well in the middle of the day wasn't simply unexpected; it was unprecedented. She would keep to herself, get her water, and get home.

But the best laid plans . . .

She approached the well, eyes averted, hoping to be on her way quickly. She stole a glance at the man, and her heart sank. He was a Jew. To Him, a woman like her would have been an outsider even among the outsiders—Samaritan, woman, and one whose reputation (deserved or not) placed her at the fringe of any group. The sooner she could be off, the better; there were few ways this could go well.

He spoke and asked for a drink.

In her shock at being spoken to, all she could manage was to give voice to that shock.

Despite the brief conversation being a bit odd— the way He spoke of living water was strange—this was going better than she could have imagined. This man was warm and caring. He didn't seem to mind the differences between them that had first concerned her. Until the conversation turned personal. He asked her to bring her husband. The uneasy and intrusive question was easily sidestepped. "I have no husband." Painful but true.

What He said next tightened her chest and

turned her stomach. He knew. He knew about her, and not just her present, but her past as well. Knowing her man was not her husband was surprising, but not completely implausible. But how did He know about her past? Did He know the full story? Did He know how she felt being in her sixth relationship? Did she know how and why they all ended? The sacrifices she was making for her own physical, mental, and emotional security?

She was too afraid to ask if He knew the answers to those questions. He was clearly a prophet, and so He may well have, and the thought of bringing those issues into open conversation was like opening a mortal wound, so she turned the conversation to religion.

In the course of their conversation, she learned He did know her. He knew her like no one else did. And He revealed why: He was the Messiah! She was sitting at a well, sharing a conversation with a man who claimed to be the Promised One, and from what He knew about her, she wondered if it might just be possible.

She went back to town. Her usual fear of interacting with her neighbors forgotten in the excitement of meeting the man who waited at the well. She told them about Him. She told them all, and she told them that He knew her story. What a thrill for her, the outsider to the outsiders, to bring this news to her village. It ignited a long-forgotten sense of purpose and importance.

Her words, her testimony about the man at the well, brought a spark of faith to many in her village. But it was not her words alone. Jesus spent two days teaching the people, and a great number of them became believers. They told the woman it was no longer simply because of her words, but because of His too.

They came to her to tell her of their faith in the Savior of the world. The people whom she used to avoid, whom she knew used to cast pitying glances toward her and speak unkind words about her, now came to her. Because of Jesus, she found a new place in the community and a new faith in the Messiah.

REFLECT

We don't know the full story of the woman at the well. But Jesus did. He knows all of our stories too—the parts we tell and the parts we try to hide. Are there parts of your life you would prefer Jesus did not expose? What would it mean to you to accept and embrace the fact that Jesus already knows those parts of your story and accepts you just the same? When was the last time you ran to tell others about Jesus? Do you know anyone who doesn't already know Him? If this woman, who was ostracized by her village, can reach out to those who scorned her, what holds you back from sharing the good news of Jesus with others?

———

Jesus, You know the details of our lives that we may have forgotten. You can tell us everything we ever did. And yet You long to sit and have a conversation with us and tell us that You are the Messiah, the one who has come to offer God's salvation to the world.

I confess that sometimes I try to keep myself hidden from You. I confess that there are parts of my life I try to hide. Forgive me for hiding from You. Give me the strength and the courage to run to my own village, to share with others the good news of Your coming, the good news of Your love for us, no matter what our stories may be. Help me to overcome the fear that sometimes holds me back from interacting with others so that they too may see and know You as Savior. Amen.

5

THE OBEDIENT

Luke 5:1–11

One day as Jesus was standing by the Lake of Gennesaret, the people were crowding around him and listening to the word of God. He saw at the water's edge two boats, left there by the fishermen, who were washing their nets. He got into one of the boats, the one belonging to Simon, and asked him to put out a little from shore. Then he sat down and taught the people from the boat.

When he had finished speaking, he said to Simon, "Put out into deep water, and let down the nets for a catch."

Simon answered, "Master, we've worked hard all night and haven't caught anything. But because you say so, I will let down the nets."

When they had done so, they caught such a large number of fish that their nets began to break. So they signaled their partners in the other boat to come and help them, and they came and filled both boats so full that they began to sink.

When Simon Peter saw this, he fell at Jesus' knees and said, "Go away from me, Lord; I am a sinful man!" For he and all his companions were astonished at the catch of fish they had taken, and so were James and John, the sons of Zebedee, Simon's partners.

Then Jesus said to Simon, "Don't be afraid; from now on you will fish for people." So they pulled their boats up on shore, left everything and followed him.

Simon stared at the net as he washed it. He saw the few small holes and wondered if any fish, however small, had escaped. Galilee was usually productive; he knew the places where fish liked to school. They had sailed to nearly a dozen of them last night. Nothing.

He'd had nights like this before. Not many, but a few. Enough to know his father would be frustrated. Simon understood. No fish meant no market. No market, no money. One day was not a disaster, but every fisherman was a bit superstitious, and the one bad night spawned fears of another.

The words of the teacher and the distraction of the crowd helped. This teacher was enchanting. He was different than the teachers Simon usually heard in the synagogue. This was not an explanation of the law; this man was painting a picture of the kingdom of heaven, of God their Father. Simon found himself working slower and slower as he listened.

The crowd was pressing closer to Jesus, who had already been crowded right to the water's edge. Looking around, He saw the boat. Without a word, He climbed in and asked Simon to put out from shore.

Jesus stood in the bow and spoke to the people. Simon watched the water as he listened. He found himself reflecting about his life. He was happy. He enjoyed fishing. It was familiar. Fishing was straightforward, uncomplicated. Listening to this teacher was stirring, but it had an air of complication to it, as though hearing too much would upset his simple life. So he let his mind wander. He thought about his next fishing trip. What was tonight's weather? Where were the fish?

Jesus was still speaking, but Simon suddenly realized Jesus was looking at him; He was speaking directly to him: "Put out into deep water, and let down the nets for a catch."

Peter sighed. He did not want to fish anymore today. But he did not want to disappoint this teacher. Something about that realization bothered him. There was only one other person he felt that way about—his father. Still, the feeling was real, and he could not deny it. "Master, we've worked hard all night and haven't caught anything. But because you say so, I will let down the nets."

They weren't even in a good fishing spot. Peter thought a quick drop and no fish was the fastest way to get back to the shore and home.

The net hadn't even fully untangled before Peter felt the first tug of fish. He chuckled to himself. *One random fish.* Another tug, this time stronger. *OK, maybe a big fish.* A big fish was always fun. Soon it was clear there was more than one fish. The net was alive with fish. Peter and his companions laughed as they struggled to pull up the net. But the laughter died when the struggle became too much. Strings and knots snapped and popped as muscles strained to lift the mass of wriggling fish, the opposing forces nearly too much for the nets.

James and John, Simon's partners, were on the shore. He called to them for help. Together, they pulled the nets in. There would be more repair work on the nets, but none of them minded. They filled their boats with the catch. The boat was noticeably lower in the water. Fortunately, shore was not far off.

In a few short minutes, the crew had their biggest catch ever.

Simon looked at Jesus. All of them did. Only Simon spoke. From his knees in the bottom of the boat, he nearly wailed, "Go away from me, Lord; I am a sinful man!" The teacher's words and this miraculous catch of fish left no doubt that this man was from God. Simon's previous exhilaration at new teaching had become shame over his life. He was a simple, and sinful, fisherman. How could he stand in the presence of a man of God?

Jesus gazed at him with a look that would, in

time, grow familiar to Simon. He reassured him that he would still be a fisherman. Only from now on he would catch men.

Simon didn't understand, but he knew that the complication he had feared was about to become a reality. And that was all right with him. He would follow this man anywhere.

REFLECT

Sometimes experience gets in the way of listening to the voice of the Lord. We know what we've tried. We know what works and what doesn't. We are the masters of our own practice. What keeps you from hearing what Jesus is asking? When did you last have a revelation of who Jesus truly is? How did you respond? How would you respond if Jesus called you to change everything? How would you know that He was doing so?

Jesus, You come to us in the familiar and offer us a different experience—different because You are there. In Your presence, life is renewed and changed.

Forgive me for remaining the same when You call me into something different. Help me to see You for who You are, even when You reveal Yourself in ways we do not expect. You have called me to be a fisher of men. Grant me the wisdom to know when to let down my net for a catch, even though I may be physically and emotionally tired. Strengthen me to pull in the bounty You provide. Amen.

6

THE HOPEFUL

Matthew 8:1–4

When Jesus came down from the mountainside, large crowds followed him. A man with leprosy came and knelt before him and said, "Lord, if you are willing, you can make me clean."

Jesus reached out his hand and touched the man. "I am willing," he said. "Be clean!" Immediately he was cleansed of his leprosy. Then Jesus said to him, "See that you don't tell anyone. But go, show yourself to the priest and offer the gift Moses commanded, as a testimony to them."

He was coming! The teacher had finished, and He was coming. The wait had seemed interminable, but that's how hopeful waiting always feels. But the wait, confining as it had been, was not without its enjoyable moments. He had stood at a distance on account of his condition, listening, thinking, trying to understand what was being said. So much had a familiar feel, yet the scene was startlingly new.

Jesus's words were powerful, full of hope, tinged with the challenge of what it meant to be one of God's people. He was adding layers of depth to the words of the law, showing their truest intent. He was not disputing the law. In a sense, He was defending it, showing its goodness, its correctness, but also its limitations to deal with sin. Jesus suggested that the laws were not simply a guide to behavior, but were given to shape the character of the Lord's people. God was not interested in hollow obedience. He wanted people whose character reflected His own, and the law was a tool to that end.

Here he stood, obeying those very laws he had just heard Jesus deepen and expand. The law required him, in his condition, to stay away from people, so he kept his distance—always. His leprosy was the defining element of his life. It dictated his social life, his wardrobe, and even his vocabulary. He wanted a cure. He missed his family and friends; he missed the temple and his God.

A miracle cure was his greatest, and perhaps his only, hope.

Coming toward him, a crowd in tow, was the man on whom that hope rested. Jesus, the man who had already healed so many, was now heading his way.

This was his moment. Leprosy required him to shout, "Unclean! Unclean!" Hope demanded that he plead for mercy. Leprosy necessitated distance from everyone. Hope pushed him straight to Jesus. If he was going to violate the restrictions of his disease, he would do so with gusto. His hope grew as the distance between himself and Jesus shrank.

It was the crowd who alerted Jesus to the unclean. He was easily recognized for what he was. The torn clothes, the tousled and unkempt hair, the mask over the lower part of his face, and his separation from the crowd all proclaimed his leprosy as clearly as if he were on the mountainside yelling about his disease to the people below.

Jesus let him come. Fearing contamination by his uncleanness, the people pulled back a step for each step he took forward. He saw their revulsion and didn't care, his hope of being restored propelling his feet forward.

The man's excitement did not overwhelm him. Stopping just short of touching Jesus, but still in clear violation of the law, he fell to his knees. The crowd faded. He could hear the cacophony of their objections, but their distance and his focus combined to make them merely background noise, inconsequential.

The leper knew Jesus was more than just a man. The power of God was at work in Him, and it was that power that the leper needed, so he spoke to Jesus as one seeking divine aid. "Lord, if you are willing, you can make me clean." He delivered the line effortlessly, a reflection of the hours he had spent rehearsing this scene in his mind. He was humble, contrite, nearly begging. His life hinged on this interaction.

He had been a leper for a long time. He suffered from both the disease and the isolation that came with the disease. Neither treatment nor time had healed him. Now he knelt in front of the one who had healed others. His hope and his desperation were on naked display.

This is where his rehearsals had stopped. He had fantasized about what *might* happen next, but he was unprepared for the reality. He expected Jesus to speak, but He did not.

There, kneeling before the miracle worker, head bowed and waiting silently, he caught his breath as a hand touched his shoulder. The forgotten feeling startled him for a moment before Jesus spoke. "I am willing. Be clean."

The leper, no longer leprous, felt the disease leave him as if his body had exhaled it. Instead of Jesus being contaminated by his touch, the man was healed. In line with the affirmations of the law Jesus had just preached, He ordered the man to see the priest and offer what the law required.

Jesus's final instructions were to tell no one what had happened to him. The man was on the verge of joyous laughter, and those instructions nearly pushed him over the edge. He would follow the instructions to the letter, but he knew that word would spread all the same. His very presence and appearance would announce his miracle. His realized hope would spread to the world around him.

REFLECT

The leprous man placed his hope in Jesus. He knew Jesus could provide, yet in his request, he maintained his humility. Both the power and the prerogative belonged to Jesus, and the leper realized that. When you approach Jesus with a request, how do you ensure that you are remaining humble while being confident in the power that Jesus has to grant your request? The leper shows us what it means to honor God while pursuing Him. Have you ever had to push the barriers of what's considered acceptable? How did you make that decision?

Jesus, Healer, thank You for being a Savior who shows compassion, who reaches out to touch us and cleanse us with Your holiness.

Forgive us for the times when we don't seek You diligently. Forgive us for relying on ourselves to supply our needs.

Help me remember that Yours is the power and the will to heal and provide. Strengthen me to rest comfortably in your will and Your decisions about my healing. And when You do act, help me to respond appropriately. May my life reflect what You have done for me. Amen.

7

THE SEEKER

Mark 2:1–12

A few days later, when Jesus again entered Capernaum, the people heard that he had come home. They gathered in such large numbers that there was no room left, not even outside the door, and he preached the word to them. Some men came, bringing to him a paralyzed man, carried by four of them. Since they could not get him to Jesus because of the crowd, they made an opening in the roof above Jesus by digging through it and then lowered the mat the man was lying on. When Jesus saw their faith, he said to the paralyzed man, "Son, your sins are forgiven."

Now some teachers of the law were sitting there, thinking to themselves, "Why does this fellow talk like that? He's blaspheming! Who can forgive sins but God alone?"

Immediately Jesus knew in his spirit that this was what they were thinking in their hearts, and he said to them, "Why are you thinking these things? Which is easier: to say to this paralyzed man, 'Your sins are forgiven,' or to say, 'Get up, take your mat and walk'? But I want you to know that the Son of Man has authority on earth to forgive sins." So he said to the man, "I tell you, get up, take your mat and go home." He got up, took his mat and walked out in full view of them all. This amazed everyone and they praised God, saying, "We have never seen anything like this!"

The crowd was nothing new. Jesus had undoubtedly earned His reputation. Healings, exorcisms, authoritative teaching—that kind of news spreads pretty quickly. The packed house was the least surprising part of the day.

Jesus stood in the middle of the room, facing the doorway, so that the people gathered outside could hear Him. His preaching was wonderful. There was an urgency and sincerity in Jesus that gave life to His teaching, life that the rabbis' words didn't have.

A faint scratching coming from the ceiling was the first hint something unusual was about to happen. Everyone, including Jesus, tried to ignore it, but then the first bits of debris fell and rattled across the floor. Jesus moved as pieces landed in his hair. More dirt hit the floor and a spot of light appeared. Then a face in the growing hole. Eyes watched the ceiling while ears listened to Jesus's words.

Finally, the hole was big enough; it darkened as an object filled it. Little by little the shape descended. It was a man. Everyone stared, but *his* eyes focused only on Jesus. The man was clearly paralyzed. It wasn't hard to guess what he wanted.

At last, the man and his mat rested on the floor. Jesus looked at him, then through the hole at his friends. He saw something that brought a small smile to his face.

"Son, your sins are forgiven."

There was a moment before the collective breathing began again. The expectant hope of the man on the mat and his friends wilted. *That's not why we're here. Of all the things we need, that was low on the list. We have sacrifices for that!*

Some teachers of the law were mingling with the crowd. The absurdity of Jesus's statement was shocking—*Who can forgive sins but God alone? This man is crazy, or worse—a blasphemer!*

As if forgiving sins wasn't sufficiently shocking, Jesus read the thoughts of the teachers and asked them why they thought He was blaspheming. The answer to that seemed obvious: He was claiming to do what only God can do; He was claiming to be God.

"Is it easier to say sins are forgiven?" Jesus said, sweeping His hand toward the crippled man, "or to tell him to walk?"

It's easier to say the former; there's no way to disprove it. No one can look into the soul and see if the sins are still there. Telling the crippled man to get up and walk is immensely more difficult.

But if Jesus can do the harder thing—tell the man to walk—then He must also have the power to forgive sins.

Jesus turned back to the man on the floor, "Get up, take your mat, and go home." Immediately, atrophied muscles grew strong. Tendons and ligaments that had shrunk and hardened from nonuse stretched to perfect length and elasticity. No therapy to ease into life on two feet. There was no pacing himself. He was up and walking, antsy to run, tempted to dance.

To the crowd, the man carrying the pallet, squeezing his way through to the door, meant something significant. "We have never seen anything like this!" they whispered among themselves. Miracles weren't new. The Jewish Scriptures were full of miracles. The people in the crowd may not have seen one before, but they knew Jesus's reputation. The real surprise was the forgiveness and its implications.

But what did it mean? What did it mean that Jesus connected healing with the forgiveness of sins? If the reality of the one implied the truth of the other, and the teachers weren't wrong that only God could forgive, then who was Jesus? The formerly crippled man *was* walking away. Heads turned from Jesus to the man and back again.

No one thought they would be encountering God that day. They all came looking for something—teaching, healing, exorcism. Some probably thought Jesus was connected to God in the same way the prophets were, but it's unlikely that any of them came expecting to literally see God. They came for Jesus; they came for miracles, for teaching. What they got was God.

REFLECT

Imagine you are the healed man. What is it like when you rejoin the friends who carried you to see Jesus—laughing and jumping, perhaps running toward home? How long before you stop walking? How long before you sit down?

When do Jesus's first words come back to you? It's clear what a difference your new legs make. What difference does forgiveness make? Does forgiveness ever become the more important miracle? Does each step remind you of the newness Jesus gave you?

Our forgiveness is the most important miracle Jesus performs for any of us. How do you celebrate and remember your forgiveness?

Jesus, when we truly meet You, we experience the miracle of forgiveness. Sometimes, we forget what You did for us first, because we are celebrating what You have done for us most recently. As time goes by, we may even forget the magnitude of the miracle of forgiveness, or maybe we realize we never really understood it in the first place.

Lord, I often forget that the most significant thing You have done for me is to forgive my sins and make me right with You. Thank You for forgiving my sin. [Be specific here.] Forgiveness is like walking home on new legs. Life will never be the same. But sometimes I don't live like a person whose legs have been healed. Help me to understand my sin and Your forgiveness so that I can celebrate and live like the healed person I am. Amen.

THE
OFFENDED

Matthew 9:9–13

As Jesus went on from there, he saw a man named Matthew sitting at the tax collector's booth. "Follow me," he told him, and Matthew got up and followed him.

While Jesus was having dinner at Matthew's house, many tax collectors and sinners came and ate with him and his disciples. When the Pharisees saw this, they asked his disciples, "Why does your teacher eat with tax collectors and sinners?"

On hearing this, Jesus said, "It is not the healthy who need a doctor, but the sick. But go and learn what this means: 'I desire mercy, not sacrifice.' For I have not come to call the righteous, but sinners."

The offense was so great that, to the onlookers, who were standing aghast and incredulous outside the house, it seemed it had to be intentional. A crowd, though not the kind that any respectable person wanted to be a part of, was lounging, laughing, and dining together. And the crowd was growing.

The home was Jewish, one that everyone knew, and most despised. It was big, of course. Its owner made a lot of money. In an act that labeled him a bona fide traitor, he took a job with the Romans and acted as an agent of their oppression. Matthew was a tax collector, and he was not a popular person.

And here was Jesus, whose actions had raised a few eyebrows already, sitting next to the traitor, eating his food, and welcoming other traitors and sinners to sit and eat. This kind of thing was just not done.

Jesus, the new teacher on the scene, the one whose healing and preaching brought amazement wherever He went, had just invited Matthew to be one of His close followers. What had started off with some curious choices—uneducated fishermen—had just taken an offensive turn. It almost seemed to be a whim. Walking past the tax office, Jesus looked in at Matthew and uttered two simple words, "Follow me."

How could the man preaching the coming of the kingdom of God invite this traitor to follow Him? Tax collectors had turned their backs on God's people. They had swapped any allegiance to God and His people for the promise of wealth from an enemy actively working against God's promises. Matthew had given up on the promises made by the God of Abraham, Isaac, and Jacob. He had rejected the law of the Lord in favor of the law of the land. And he benefited from this choice. While he was not liked, he was not lacking. If his neighbors didn't know what he did for a living, they might have thought God's blessing was upon him.

To the pious Pharisees, watching from outside so they didn't contaminate themselves, Matthew was unclean and wholly offensive. They stood in judgment, as confusion over the revelry slipped into offense and outrage, their imagination tracking the contamination as it spread from person to person, unclean hand to unclean hand.

Finally, with the wave of people entering the

house, the offense crested and burst their mental dam. Grabbing one of Jesus's disciples, one of them asked, "Why does your teacher eat with tax collectors and sinners?" The question wasn't one of curiosity; it came from a place of disbelief, indignation, offense, frustration—every emotion that surfaces when standards are violated by someone expected to uphold them.

Jesus had heard the question, so He turned His attention from those who wanted it, away from the "tax collectors and sinners," the unclean outcasts, despised and rejected. His reply was enigmatic and double-edged: "It is not the healthy who need a doctor, but the sick. But go and learn what this means: 'I desire mercy, not sacrifice.' For I have not come to call the righteous, but sinners."

Acknowledging the status of both groups, the healthy and the sick, the righteous and the sinners, Jesus agreed, in part, with the Pharisees. Those gathered around the table with Him were sick; they needed the compassion and healing hand of a doctor. The merrymakers were sinners who needed to be called back to God.

But Jesus's words cut both ways. Jesus was

being doctor and prophet to the hurting and lost, and He was telling the Pharisees they should have been doing the same. In comparison to the sick and the sinners, the Pharisees were healthy and righteous, but in reality they were neither truly healthy nor truly righteous. They were not, in fact, doing what God desired. They were not acting in mercy. The tax collectors were hurting the finances of their own people, and the Pharisees were hurting their souls.

From the festivities of His shared meal, during which Jesus invited the sick to come and get well, He offered an open door to those who were offended by His actions. Jesus knew both groups needed His healing, and He offered it to them. With those who had been ostracized, He socialized. With those who revered the law and the will of God, He invited them to study the Scriptures on a deeper level to discover what God truly desires.

REFLECT

It's easy to be offended. Our sin-broken world is filled with actions that deserve our offense. We are also offended by things that challenge our accepted social norms. Then there are offenses that arise when someone tramples on one of our passions or beliefs. It is difficult to watch someone flout what we hold dear, to see them disregard what we work so hard to safeguard and live by. It is particularly difficult when the offending person claims to believe the same things we do. Are there offenses that you see causing rifts in your relationships? Are you willing to hear that perhaps the grounds for your offense are your own misunderstandings? How do you respond to Jesus's challenge to understand God's desires for you more deeply?

Jesus, we are grateful that You came to call sinners to repentance and to heal the sick. We know we need your healing touch, to hear your call to grieve our sins and come back to the Father. Thank You for reaching out to those no one else would welcome. Thank You for showing that no one was—and that no one is—beyond the reach of Your grace and compassion.

I confess that my confidence in my own understanding sets me up as judge over others whose understanding may differ. I know You call Your followers to be healers for a hurting world by bringing Your love to them. I confess that sometimes it's easier to stand at a distance and judge "the sick," and even those who reach out to them, rather than offer mercy. Help me to understand mercy over sacrifice and healing over piety. Forgive me for failing to offer to others what has been freely given to me. Help me to reach out to those who need a hand. Amen.

9

THE BROKEN

John 5:1–14

Some time later, Jesus went up to Jerusalem for one of the Jewish festivals. Now there is in Jerusalem near the Sheep Gate a pool, which in Aramaic is called Bethesda and which is surrounded by five covered colonnades. Here a great number of disabled people used to lie— the blind, the lame, the paralyzed. One who was there had been an invalid for thirty-eight years. When Jesus saw him lying there and learned that he had been in this condition for a long time, he asked him, "Do you want to get well?"

"Sir," the invalid replied, "I have no one to help me into the pool when the water is stirred.

While I am trying to get in, someone else goes down ahead of me."

Then Jesus said to him, "Get up! Pick up your mat and walk." At once the man was cured; he picked up his mat and walked. The day on which this took place was a Sabbath, and so the Jewish leaders said to the man who had been healed, "It is the Sabbath; the law forbids you to carry your mat."

But he replied, "The man who made me well said to me, 'Pick up your mat and walk.'"

So they asked him, "Who is this fellow who told you to pick it up and walk?"

The man who was healed had no idea who it was, for Jesus had slipped away into the crowd that was there.

Later Jesus found him at the temple and said to him, "See, you are well again. Stop sinning or something worse may happen to you." The man went away and told the Jewish leaders that it was Jesus who had made him well.

The question was slightly odd. It suggested there was a possibility the answer might be negative, that indeed he did not want to be well—which, of course, he did want. That is why he spent his days here by the pool, waiting for the waters to be stirred, trying to be the first one in.

He had been coming to this pool for a long time, not as long as he had been an invalid—that particular time frame was thirty-eight years. He'd been without the use of his legs far longer than he had walked. Still, he had been coming to this pool for nearly as long as his legs had been useless. It had been a long time to hold on to hope, a long time of trying to win the race to the stirred waters and immerse himself in the healing current.

In his more honest moments, he knew he was simply coming to the pool because it was a good place to beg. He could not run from the reality that his arms were not strong enough to compete with healthy legs. He wanted the pool. Perhaps one day he would be the only one present when the waters churned and there would be no race; he could pull himself in with his arms and walk out on his healed legs. Someday. Maybe.

The paralyzed man looked up at the man who

had asked him if he wanted to be well. "I have no one to help me into the pool when the water is stirred. While I am trying to get in, someone else goes down ahead of me."

The man looked directly at him. Eyes held. The standing man uttered an unforgettable command. "Get up! Pick up your mat and walk."

A long-forgotten feeling of strength flooded his legs. By the time he had understood the words, the ability to carry them out had been restored. Muscles filled and flexed, tendons stretched and tightened, nerves prickled. The formerly paralyzed man did as instructed. He stood up. He picked up his mat. He walked.

It was the Sabbath, a day to rest, to celebrate God's work—of creation and re-creation, and of liberation.

Over the centuries, since the Sabbath command was originally given at Sinai, specifics of how one did (and perhaps more importantly did not) honor the Sabbath had developed. There were definitions and strict guidelines to follow.

But the Sabbath and its proper observance were far from the formerly paralyzed man's mind. The mat was no burden to transport in his hands. The man who had restored the ability to take the mat anywhere had told him to carry it. He was doing just that. And it was wonderful.

While no burden to him, the Pharisees saw his mat differently. It was a burden; it was work, and it broke the Sabbath. His sin could not be allowed. Their chastisement, however, did not dissuade the healed man. "The man who made me well said to me, 'Pick up your mat and walk.'" So that is what he did, and that is what he intended to continue doing.

The Pharisees were astonished that someone had instructed him to break the law. Who would encourage deliberate sin? But the man did not know. His healer had slipped quietly into the crowd after restoring the use of his legs.

It was only later that he learned the identity of his healer. It was Jesus. Sometime later, Jesus found him at the temple, still carrying his mat. The object in his hand a testimony to his newfound connection to his healer.

Jesus's final words struck a note that caused the man to rethink the last thirty-eight years of his life and set the tone for whatever years lay ahead of him. "See, you are well again. Stop sinning or something worse may happen to you."

REFLECT

The man who had been paralyzed had one response to Jesus that found multiple expressions. He responded in faith and that led to obedience and testimony. He did not put down the mat, and he told those who wanted to know who had done this thing for him. Do those two characteristics describe you? Jesus does not ask us to do anything before He heals us, but once we have received His healing and forgiveness, a response is necessary. Does your life reflect the gratitude that His kindness deserves? Have you left behind your life of sin to follow the One who has healed you?

Jesus, You know us intimately. You know our past, present, and future. Thank You that You come to us and ask if we want to be made well. Forgive us for taking the gift of spiritual healing and then simply living for ourselves. Empower us to live as part of Your family.

71

Help me to respond in obedience and to broadcast what you have done for me to everyone who asks. Help me to take the mat You have delivered me from and carry it as a badge of pride that shows the world who has healed me. Amen.

THE SELF-RIGHTEOUS

10

Mark 3:1–6

Another time Jesus went into the synagogue, and a man with a shriveled hand was there. Some of them were looking for a reason to accuse Jesus, so they watched him closely to see if he would heal him on the Sabbath. Jesus said to the man with the shriveled hand, "Stand up in front of everyone."

Then Jesus asked them, "Which is lawful on the Sabbath: to do good or to do evil, to save life or to kill?" But they remained silent.

He looked around at them in anger and, deeply distressed at their stubborn hearts, said to the man, "Stretch out your hand." He stretched it out, and his hand was completely restored.

> Then the Pharisees went out and began to plot
> with the Herodians how they might kill Jesus.

They were all there, sitting in their places of prominence, relishing the honor the people gave them. They had earned their seats. The synagogue was their house; the people, their charge; the law of God, their guide. They sat, pleased with themselves, believing God was pleased with them.

Then He walked in. No one had made such a commotion in so short a time, at least not in living memory. He had been the topic of much conversation already. Who was He? What was He doing? What was His purpose? His teaching stretched the boundaries, indeed broke them. If that were all He was doing, He wouldn't be such a conundrum, but the power that was clearly at His disposal made it difficult to deny He was sent from God. For the Pharisees, Jesus was a problem.

Everyone watched Him as He entered. He surveyed those in attendance. He noted each one. Then His eyes held. He saw a man with a shriveled hand. Several pharisaical eyebrows raised. It was the Sabbath. What would Jesus do? Healing was considered work, even if the labor involved was nothing more than speaking. To them, it was accomplishing a task that could wait until the holy day was over that mattered, not the mechanics of the deed. Would Jesus work on the Sabbath?

Jesus called the man to the front. Surely, He was about to do something. He spoke, not to the man, but to the crowd, to the Pharisees and teachers of the law. The man they thought would serve as a test for Jesus had now turned into a test for them. "Which is lawful on the Sabbath: to do good or to do evil, to save life or to kill?"

They knew the answer to the question. It was not a trick, but it was a trap. The answer was obvious from both sides. Doing evil or taking a life was never okay, Sabbath or not. The only other option he gave them was doing good, saving life. How could that ever be truly unlawful?

They knew that honoring the Sabbath was based in the dual grounding of God's work of creation and God's freeing the Israelites from slavery. If being rescued from bondage was reason to celebrate, then certainly releasing another person from bondage was a proper celebration. Giving, restoring life was not a violation of the Sabbath; it was perhaps the truest way to honor it. But to admit that would be to give license to Jesus. So they remained silent, and they waited.

The silence stretched. As it grew, so did Jesus's anger. But Jesus would not make this man wait for the sake of their traditions. He looked at the man and decidedly, deliberately, "broke" the Sabbath. "Stretch out your hand," Jesus said, ordering something the man had not been able to do. The man raised his arm and stretched out his hand, the first time in a long time.

The man and his family were overjoyed. This healing would change all their lives. No more would they be forced to rely solely on the kindness and generosity of their community. They could provide for themselves now; they could even contribute to others in need. Those who had received for so long could now give.

The Pharisees, on the contrary, were humiliated and angry. Jesus had not simply broken their traditions. His question had exposed a weakness, and people had seen it. They had been stripped of their power, and Jesus had demonstrated His.

Jesus was no longer a problem; He was a threat. He was showing people there was another way of understanding Scripture, another way of knowing God.

If His way was right, then theirs was wrong. But they could not be wrong. They knew God; they knew the laws of Moses. They obeyed. They obeyed correctly. This could not be allowed. Something would have to be done about Jesus.

REFLECT

It is unlikely we would challenge Jesus, that we would put our knowledge and practice up against His. But we may challenge each other on what Scripture means and how to properly honor God with its application. Sometimes, this is good and necessary. But are there times when our debates and disagreements unnecessarily cause division? How do you interact with those who understand, interpret, or (especially) apply Scripture differently than you do? What about those who claim the name of Jesus and yet are on the other side of a social issue? Does your grip on your position preclude you from reaching out to others?

———————

Jesus, we know it is in our nature to seek out the truth and come to conclusions on various issues, whether they be theological or social. But You never intended us to use our positions as a club with which to assault others. Forgive us for our arrogance. Forgive us for judging others unfairly. Help us to be gracious with those whose interpretations of Scripture differ from ours.

Forgive me for the times that my faith, my understanding of what I should do, has actually withheld life from someone else. Forgive me for the times I have been a barrier to You instead of a bridge. Help me to hold fast to the good and to release all else. Amen.

11

THE UNINITIATED

Matthew 8:5–13

When Jesus had entered Capernaum, a centurion came to him, asking for help. "Lord," he said, "my servant lies at home paralyzed, suffering terribly."

Jesus said to him, "Shall I come and heal him?"

The centurion replied, "Lord, I do not deserve to have you come under my roof. But just say the word, and my servant will be healed. For I myself am a man under authority, with soldiers under me. I tell this one, 'Go,' and he goes; and that one, 'Come,' and he comes. I say to my servant, 'Do this,' and he does it."

When Jesus heard this, he was amazed and said to those following him, "Truly I tell you, I have not found anyone in Israel with such great faith.

I say to you that many will come from the east and the west, and will take their places at the feast with Abraham, Isaac and Jacob in the kingdom of heaven. But the subjects of the kingdom will be thrown outside, into the darkness, where there will be weeping and gnashing of teeth."

Then Jesus said to the centurion, "Go! Let it be done just as you believed it would." And his servant was healed at that moment.

It was good to be coming home, at least to a home base. Capernaum was a familiar town for Jesus and His disciples.

A familiar refrain could be heard rolling through the crowds, "Nothing like this has ever been seen in Israel." It had indeed been a long time since God had sent a miracle-working messenger to His people. Yet here, in their presence, was someone proclaiming the kingdom of God, and His words and deeds revealed that He carried God's authority. Without it, the demons would have defied Him and diseases would have run their destructive and deadly course. But with a touch or a word, demons departed, leprosy vanished, blind eyes opened, and withered limbs strengthened.

Entering the city, Jesus was met by a centurion. He walked confidently toward Jesus, determination set in his features. But when he reached Jesus, his faced softened in concern. "Lord," he said, "my servant lies at home paralyzed, suffering terribly." With the first word, the disciples were lost.

A Roman, a centurion, a leader of Roman soldiers, stood before Jesus showing both respect and deference. He called Jesus *Lord*, a term used in submission, often used by the faithful when asking God for help.

If Jesus was surprised, as His disciples clearly were, He did not show it. He merely suggested that He come to the centurion's home and heal the servant. He started to walk, but the centurion stopped Him.

"Lord—." There was that term again. He must have known what he was saying. This Roman soldier showed more respect to Jesus than many of Jesus's own people.

The centurion didn't need to have Jesus come to his home. He knew that Jesus had both the power and the authority to heal with a word and from a distance. Jesus did not need to come and see the servant, but merely to say the word and it would be done. Just as the centurion would give an order and it would be carried about by those under his command, Jesus could give the order and it would be done just as He commanded.

If the disciples were amazed that this man would refer to Jesus as Lord, Jesus Himself was amazed at the faith and understanding of this foreigner. He marveled aloud at the centurion's faith, telling those gathered that He had not seen any faith in Israel that rivaled this man's.

At this, many eyes in the crowd dropped. They had been following Jesus for the show, hoping to get something for their own personal gain. Few had actually shown any real faith in Jesus. But Jesus was not satisfied with highlighting this man's beautiful faith and chastising the crowd for their lack of it. He went on. Outsiders would be welcomed into the kingdom of God while many of the children of Israel would be left outside!

A centurion's display of faith had prompted Jesus to proclaim a great reversal. Jews were the descendants of Abraham, inheritors of the promises and the covenants. They were the ones waiting for Messiah and God's kingdom, and now they would be left outside the feast? Why would the faith of an outsider allow him admittance to the kingdom while a son of the covenant would be kept from it?

Faith. The correlation was clear. On one side were the centurion (an outsider), his faith, and the kingdom of God. On the other were the people of Israel (the insiders), their lack of faith, and being left outside. Faith—faith in Jesus and His authority—was the key to entrance into the kingdom of God. Faith brought the outsiders in; a lack of faith pushed the insiders out.

As confirmation of the centurion's place at the feast, Jesus said to the him, "Go! Let it be done just as you believed it would."

The centurion returned home to find his servant well, as though he had never suffered. The crowd, however, had taken on a kind of suffering of its own. Jesus's words were uttered in earnest and had the impact of both warning and threat. They went home and wondered at the idea of the importance of faith and, in comparison, the insignificance of their heritage.

REFLECT

Perhaps you consider your faith mature and well established. But have you ever been impressed with the words and deeds of someone who is a new follower of Christ? Ever wondered why your faith doesn't look as active, vibrant, or trusting as theirs? Why would it be that someone young in their Christian walk would show stronger, deeper, more dedicated faith than a person who has followed Jesus for a long time? When was the last time you truly acted on your faith? Under what circumstances did you do, or even say, something that reflected your belief in the power and authority of Jesus?

Jesus, You are the object of our faith. You are the one who lived and died for us. We are grateful for the sacrifice you made and the invitation to trust You. But sometimes our faith is narrow and weak. Sometimes we do not act in faith or trust You as the one who has all power and authority. Forgive us for having such small faith. Forgive us for living as though Your power is no longer at work in the world. We do not always expect the miracle, but we know that Yours is the power to accomplish it.

You have called me to live in the faith that I profess. Help me to live today in the strength of true faith, knowing it is faith in You that reserves my place at the feast in the kingdom of heaven. Amen.

12

THE VULNERABLE

Luke 7:11–17

Soon afterward, Jesus went to a town called Nain, and his disciples and a large crowd went along with him. As he approached the town gate, a dead person was being carried out—the only son of his mother, and she was a widow. And a large crowd from the town was with her. When the Lord saw her, his heart went out to her and he said, "Don't cry."

Then he went up and touched the bier they were carrying him on, and the bearers stood still. He said, "Young man, I say to you, get up!" The dead man sat up and began to talk, and Jesus gave him back to his mother.

They were all filled with awe and praised God. "A great prophet has appeared among us,"

they said. "God has come to help his people."
This news about Jesus spread throughout Judea
and the surrounding country.

As the crowd drew near the small village, they
saw a large group of people emerging from
the town; it was soon evident this was a funeral
procession. The Jewish practice of burying the
dead quickly suggested that the loss was a recent
and very raw event. The sounds of grief reached
the group at nearly the same moment the men
emerged carrying the body.

The crowd stopped as the mourners drew near.
The two groups coalesced around the grief of
death, sharing in the sense of loss.

A widow walked among the mourners. Many
in Jesus's crowd assumed that the body was that
of her husband. But it was revealed that her husband
had already died. Here on the plank was
her only son. She was now alone.

The sense of grief deepened. To be alone, a
widow with no son, was a precarious and vulnerable
place to be. The minds of Jesus's followers
recalled the laws of Moses, the requirements
given to care for and protect widows. This

woman was now alone and her care, her very life, depended on those around her obeying the laws of Moses, the laws that Jesus preached and expounded upon. Each person in the crowd felt a deep sense of responsibility. A general curiosity wound its way through the mass following Jesus: What would He say about taking care of widows?

So much of what He had already said about the law had stretched its meaning. It was not enough simply to follow the letter of the law. More important was a person's devotion to God, from which true obedience came. Surely this wasn't different. If caring for widows by providing for their food was already a part of the law, how could that be deepened? They were not prepared for what they were about to see.

Jesus, standing at the front of the group watched as the mourners approached Him. He saw the grief of the widow as she walked solemnly and slowly next to her dead son. He knew the life that was ahead of her, a life that depended on the goodness of others, a life of toiling in the fields to gather what was left behind after the harvest. He envisioned her stooped, her back strained after hours of labor, picking the kernels of wheat. He knew the coming sore joints as she ground the wheat to make flour. He imagined the sadness and sorrow of a life spent alone, the very work of surviving a toilsome weariness. His heart went out to her. He felt compassion for her.

Jesus stepped toward the widow, and she looked up at Him. Her eyes wet with tears, face red with emotional exhaustion, her expression a mask of grief and anxiety.

"Don't cry." The words, uttered in gentility, shocked all who heard them. They seemed cruel and callous. What a thing to say to a mother wounded by the death of her only son! The grieving woman flinched. How could she do anything but cry? The loss of a child is enough to crush any parent. But to lose an only child after the death of a spouse—surely this was grief beyond what many would ever experience.

But when the woman's eyes met His, her shock faded. She saw the deep compassion and sympathy they held.

Jesus turned His head and looked at the body. He left the widow standing and walked to the bier stretched between the men carrying it. As He approached, they stopped. Many in the crowd held their breath as Jesus came dangerously close to the dead body and risked becoming ceremonially unclean.

But He did not touch. He stood next to the boy's head. Leaning forward, He spoke softly but firmly to the body. "Young man, I say to you, get up." The body, revived by the words and power of Jesus, sat up, his burial wraps stretching and straining as his body shifted positions. He began to speak.

The men quickly lowered the bier and unwrapped his head. Jesus took him and walked him back to his mother, whose tears flowed even more than before as she received her son back.

Wonder spread through both crowds. The stories of Elijah and Elisha sprang to the minds of many. Both prophets had raised widows' sons, just as Jesus had now done.

A few dwelled on the differences between what Jesus had done and the resurrections performed by the prophets of old. Compared to the work of the ancient prophets, Jesus's resurrection was startlingly easy, requiring Him only to speak. Most, however, were caught up in the joy and wonder of the moment, the comparison between Jesus and the prophets of another era finding utterance in their exclamations: "A great prophet has appeared among us," they said. "God has come to help his people."

This story spread faster than Jesus could travel. News of His words and deeds went ahead of Him.

REFLECT

Life is hard in so many ways. It often feels as though the give and take of life is terribly out of balance. What do you feel life has unfairly taken from you? How do you mourn the losses you experience? What comfort does the compassion of Jesus offer you? How do you reach out to help the destitute and vulnerable? In what ways might you be guilty of practicing the sentiments but not the actions of compassion?

Jesus, thank You for the compassion You show us and all the ways You provide for us in our times of need. We know we are surrounded by others in need—those with spiritual needs, emotional needs, physical needs, and sometimes all three.

Forgive me for the times I've been guilty of offering empty sentiments divorced from action. Help me in my efforts to practice a true and better religion as I look after those in need. Amen.

THE CONFUSED

Matthew 11:1–6

After Jesus had finished instructing his twelve disciples, he went on from there to teach and preach in the towns of Galilee.

When John, who was in prison, heard about the deeds of the Messiah, he sent his disciples to ask him, "Are you the one who is to come, or should we expect someone else?"

Jesus replied, "Go back and report to John what you hear and see: The blind receive sight, the lame walk, those who have leprosy are cleansed, the deaf hear, the dead are raised, and the good news is proclaimed to the poor. Blessed is anyone who does not stumble on account of me."

John the Baptist was in prison. John was Jesus's cousin, so he knew of Jesus's reputation and the things He was doing. John thought Jesus was the Promised One. Yet John was sitting in a jail cell. The forerunner of the Messiah was stuck in prison for doing his job.

From his cell, and in confusion, a fundamental question formed in John's mind, a question that needed an answer. The answer carried life-altering significance. John sent his disciples to ask Jesus a simple yes-or-no question: "Are you the one, or should we expect another?"

Up to this point, John seemed to know better than anyone who Jesus was. He had made an out-of-the-blue statement about Jesus being the Lamb of God who takes away the sin of the world. John even demurred to baptize Jesus, saying that it would be more appropriate for Jesus to baptize him instead. While still in his mother's womb, John seemed to react to the approach of the embryonic Jesus; John's mother exclaimed that the baby in her belly leaped for joy when Mary (pregnant with Jesus at the time) greeted her.

Yet when things went afoul of expectations,

John sent his own disciples to ask Jesus if He is indeed the Messiah. The confidence that caused John to say that Jesus was the sacrificial Lamb of God, who would take away the sin of the world had devolved into questions and confusion. Why was he confused? Why the question?

In ancient Israel, the idea of the Messiah carried with it a variety of ideas about who He would be and what He would do. Messiah was supposed to usher in God's kingdom, to set things right for Israel. The least part of that was Israel would be free again; the nation would have political independence.

How am I sitting in prison? Others are getting their miracles. The things Jesus does sound like the works of Messiah, but it doesn't make sense that I'm here. If He is who I think He is, the kingdom should be coming back to Israel—and I shouldn't be sitting here in prison. Not unreasonable thoughts to have. For John, something wasn't adding up.

John was committed to doing God's work, no matter what it cost him, but the one bringing God's kingdom had arrived! It was time for the world to change, for justice to roll down. John was wondering, Have I missed something? Is the Messiah not who I thought He was?

Jesus's response embraces the question, validates John's confusion, and offers encouragement to all those seeking answers. "Tell John what you see. The blind see, the lame walk, the lepers are healed, the deaf hear, the dead are raised, and the good news is delivered to the poor." These were signs of the coming of the kingdom of God, the arrival of the Messiah. Jesus was telling His troubled cousin, "Yes, I am the Messiah, and I am ushering in the kingdom of God; it's coming, along with every good thing that was promised."

But John was hunched in his prison cell. He never got his miracle; he was killed, and his head offered as a gift to a young girl and her mother.

At the end of Jesus's message to John the Baptist, He said, "Blessed is anyone who does not stumble on account of me." Why would anyone stumble because such good things were happening? Jesus was telling John not to give up hope in the kingdom or in the Messiah because others were experiencing the miraculous and he wasn't. Jesus's encouragement was—and still is—this: even though you may not get what you want or what you expect, it doesn't mean I am not who I said I am.

It can be difficult to accept good things for others when we want—when we *need*—some good to come our way too. We can become bitter. We can lose faith. We can decide we are better off on our own. But God is still God, even when we are confused, frustrated, disappointed, and stuck in the waiting.

REFLECT

Imagine John's certainty about Messiah and what He was supposed to do. How do you respond when Jesus doesn't seem to be doing what you think He should? What expectations do you have of Jesus? Have you ever been let down when Jesus didn't do what you wanted or expected? Have you ever wondered when it was going to be your turn to be blessed?

Jesus, we all want things. We all have expectations for the situations we face in life. Some of our desires are more selfish than others. We recognize that fact. And we also recognize that You are capable of answering each and every one of our requests. In our limited understanding, we can't always see why You do not.

I confess I am sometimes confused and disappointed that the thing I want does not become a reality. I wanted [name the thing you wanted that did not happen], and I was hurt and disappointed and confused when it did not happen. I was jealous of those who seemed to be getting the very things that I wanted. Help me to remember that You are who You are and that You still love me even when things don't seem to make sense. Amen.

14

THE DISMISSIVE

Luke 7:36–50

When one of the Pharisees invited Jesus to have dinner with him, he went to the Pharisee's house and reclined at the table. A woman in that town who lived a sinful life learned that Jesus was eating at the Pharisee's house, so she came there with an alabaster jar of perfume. As she stood behind him at his feet weeping, she began to wet his feet with her tears. Then she wiped them with her hair, kissed them and poured perfume on them.

When the Pharisee who had invited him saw this, he said to himself, "If this man were a prophet, he would know who is touching him and what kind of woman she is—that she is a sinner."

Jesus answered him, "Simon, I have something to tell you."

"Tell me, teacher," he said.

"Two people owed money to a certain moneylender. One owed him five hundred denarii, and the other fifty. Neither of them had the money to pay him back, so he forgave the debts of both. Now which of them will love him more?"

Simon replied, "I suppose the one who had the bigger debt forgiven."

"You have judged correctly," Jesus said.

Then he turned toward the woman and said to Simon, "Do you see this woman? I came into your house. You did not give me any water for my feet, but she wet my feet with her tears and wiped them with her hair. You did not give me a kiss, but this woman, from the time I entered, has not stopped kissing my feet. You did not put oil on my head, but she has poured perfume on my feet. Therefore, I tell you, her many sins have been forgiven—as her great love has shown. But whoever has been forgiven little loves little."

Then Jesus said to her, "Your sins are forgiven."

The other guests began to say among themselves, "Who is this who even forgives sins?"

Jesus said to the woman, "Your faith has
saved you; go in peace."

She was familiar. Everyone in town knew who
and what she was, the life she led. People of
Simon's class had written her off as undesirable
and unclean. She had lived her lifestyle for a
long time and showed no signs of change. Her
uncleanness made others unclean. She was, as
far as Simon was concerned, an infection, one
that could not be treated.

Her tears began to fall on Jesus's feet. Simon
winced as each drop wetted a new spot on His
feet. His heart told him the tears must burn as
they land—physically untrue, of course, but the
thought of any part of that woman coming into
contact with him made Simon nauseous. If he
could have removed her from his home without
creating an incident—a bigger scene than she
was already making—he would have done so.

When her tears had soaked Jesus's feet, she
began wiping them dry with her hair. Simon took
a deep breath and held it, insult upon insult was

being shown to his house and his guest. Finally, she took the perfume she had brought and poured it on Jesus's feet, kissing them while she did so. This most intimate gesture was the last Simon could stand; he could not believe Jesus was allowing her to touch Him and in such a familiar way.

Surely, Simon thought, this man Jesus must not know who she truly is. And if He did not, then He must not be a prophet. The thought brought a small token of consolation to an otherwise regrettable dinner.

Jesus, who had been watching the woman since she had approached, spoke to Simon without taking his eyes off the woman at His feet: "Simon, I have something to tell you."

Simon, with a subconscious eye roll and a hint of a *This-ought-to-be-good* edge to his voice, asked Him to proceed. Jesus looked at him.

The story Jesus told was simple, if slightly implausible. It featured an uncharacteristically merciful moneylender, but he was not the focus of the story. The two debtors were. Jesus asked which one would love the moneylender more. Love was perhaps a strong category for a response to loan forgiveness, but the answer was obvious, and so Simon gave it. He wondered about the purpose of this story.

The wait was not long.

Jesus returned His eyes to the woman. He then began to compare Simon and the woman! The very idea of being compared to such a sinful woman was unbelievable to Simon. Regardless of what the woman had offered Him and how many social faux pas Simon had committed, comparing a Pharisee to a woman of her low character was insulting. With each point of comparison, Simon's embarrassment and frustration grew. Everyone listening could see that what was being said was true. Simon had done none of the things He should have done for Jesus; she had done them instead.

Then Jesus offered a verdict that left the entire crowd bewildered: "Her many sins have been forgiven—as her great love has shown. But whoever has been forgiven little loves little." Then Jesus said to her, "Your sins are forgiven."

He didn't make the direct comparison between the two of them this time; He didn't need to. The meaning was plain. Simon, if he had been forgiven anything, was only forgiven little, for he had loved little.

(In the days and weeks that followed, Simon would try to convince himself that he was not in need of forgiveness, and therefore the point didn't matter. But the accusation of loving little kept stabbing at him, its implications refusing to let go of his mind or his conscience.)

Finally, mercifully, for Simon, Jesus brought the spectacle to an end. It was fitting for the situation but spectacular. Jesus said to the woman, "Your faith has saved you; go in peace."

REFLECT

In an honest moment, do you identify more with Simon or the woman? Do you show love and kindness to Jesus and others, or do you take for granted His presence and forgiveness? Do you perhaps think of yourself as not needing as much forgiveness as some others? Of course, we all need forgiveness in the same way, but sometimes it's easy to think that, practically speaking, we haven't sinned as much as others. If someone were to see your love for Jesus and others, how much would they think you have been forgiven?

Loving Savior, thank You for the forgiveness You have made possible. Thank You that Your forgiveness is generous to the point of extravagance. Sometimes we have not truly understood our forgiveness, its depth and reality.

I confess that sometimes I do not struggle with my sin, that I do not think about it in specific ways. Grant me the strength to examine myself, to recognize my need for You and Your forgiveness. Help me to accept that forgiveness and live in freedom, so others might see how You have changed me. May the forgiveness You have given me result in greater love for You and others. Amen.

15

THE PERPLEXED

Matthew 13:10–23

The disciples came to him and asked, "Why do you speak to the people in parables?"

He replied, "Because the knowledge of the secrets of the kingdom of heaven has been given to you, but not to them. Whoever has will be given more, and they will have an abundance. Whoever does not have, even what they have will be taken from them. This is why I speak to them in parables:

> "Though seeing, they do not see;
> though hearing, they do not hear or
> understand.

In them is fulfilled the prophecy of Isaiah:

> "'You will be ever hearing but never
> understanding;

you will be ever seeing but never per-
ceiving.
For this people's heart has become cal-
loused;
they hardly hear with their ears,
and they have closed their eyes.
Otherwise they might see with their eyes,
hear with their ears,
understand with their hearts
and turn, and I would heal them.'

But blessed are your eyes because they see, and
your ears because they hear. For truly I tell you,
many prophets and righteous people longed to
see what you see but did not see it, and to hear
what you hear but did not hear it.

"Listen then to what the parable of the sower
means: When anyone hears the message about
the kingdom and does not understand it, the evil
one comes and snatches away what was sown in
their heart. This is the seed sown along the path.
The seed falling on rocky ground refers to someone who hears the word and at once receives it
with joy. But since they have no root, they last
only a short time. When trouble or persecution

comes because of the word, they quickly fall away. The seed falling among the thorns refers to someone who hears the word, but the worries of this life and the deceitfulness of wealth choke the word, making it unfruitful. But the seed falling on good soil refers to someone who hears the word and understands it. This is the one who produces a crop, yielding a hundred, sixty or thirty times what was sown."

The waves tossed pebbles and bits of foam to the shore; the rhythmic sound of the water mixed with the occasional calls of the circling gulls that floated down from the sunny skies overhead.

Jesus sat in a boat looking out over the gathering people. They returned His gaze as they sat on the grass and sand to listen. What would He say? What new teaching would He offer? What explanation of the heart and laws of God would pierce their minds and grip their hearts?

Jesus began to speak.

As His voice fell over the crowd, Jesus watched as neighbors leaned into each other and whispered. "Why is he telling stories?"

"What does this have to do with the law?"

"What does this mean?"

"What are we supposed to do with this? We didn't come for story time!"

Farmers, seeds, soil, weeds, birds, scorching sunlight? The words were clear, their familiar imagery forming a picture in each listening mind. Who didn't battle the birds and the weeds? When was the scorching sun not a threat to the precious crops? Who didn't celebrate an abundant harvest and rue the difficulty of wresting food from the soil?

The meaning obscured, the crowd discussed the story. "The farmer was clearly careless. Why wouldn't he throw all the seed on the good soil?"

"What did he expect would happen to seed scattered on a path? Of course, it would get trampled; it's where people walk!"

"What a waste of seeds, to spread them where there was so much threat to their growth."

Confusion rippled through the crowd. A slight smile touched the corners of Jesus's mouth. It was what He had expected, what He had intended.

But it wasn't just the people in the crowd who were left scratching their heads. Jesus's own disciples were also wondering, not simply about the meaning of the parable but why Jesus chose to speak in such a way to begin with. "Why do you speak to the people in parables?" the question perhaps deflecting their own lack of understanding.

The disciples processed the reply. The enigma was intentional. They were not meant to understand. Hard hearts had closed eyes and stopped up ears.

Jesus, the Promised One, who was proclaiming the need for repentance because of the nearness of the kingdom of heaven was now saying that the secrets of that kingdom were hidden to some.

Confusion is difficult to mask, so Jesus explained to them what was hidden in the sower, the seeds, and the soil. The sower and the seed are the same in each sowing. It is the dirt that is different. The soil is the key to the harvest. The same plant springs up wherever it can take root, but the health and produce of the plant depends on the soil.

Jesus spoke in parables to hide the message from those not meant or not ready to receive it. The parable He told confirmed that some on whom the good seed fell would produce no harvest. Only those whose soil was without rocks, weeds, or blistering sunshine would receive the seed, see it germinate and grow, and finally produce the fruit of an incredible harvest.

REFLECT

Many stories and passages from Scripture can be difficult to understand. The distance of time and culture obscure what may have been plain to the original audience or the first readers of the Scriptures. How often do we wrestle with the words of Scripture? Do we, like the confused crowds and disciples, walk away from the words of the Lord puzzled and lacking understanding? And do we, like the disciples, ask for a clearer understanding? The explanation given to them was not given to the crowds. How do we respond when we encounter difficult words from Scripture?

Loving Father, we are grateful You have chosen to reveal Yourself in the world around us, in the

Scriptures, in the great story of redemption, and ultimately in the life and words of Jesus. Thank You for allowing us to see who You are, what You have done, and what You are still doing to bring a lost world back to You.

I confess, Lord, that I do not always understand the meaning of Your words and your ways. I do not want to rely on my own interpretations. Help me to overcome the distance of time, culture, and worldview. Like the disciples, I ask You to enlighten my understanding of the secrets of the kingdom of heaven. Amen.

16

THE RESCUED

Mark 4:35–41

That day when evening came, he said to his disciples, "Let us go over to the other side." Leaving the crowd behind, they took him along, just as he was, in the boat. There were also other boats with him. A furious squall came up, and the waves broke over the boat, so that it was nearly swamped. Jesus was in the stern, sleeping on a cushion. The disciples woke him and said to him, "Teacher, don't you care if we drown?"

He got up, rebuked the wind and said to the waves, "Quiet! Be still!" Then the wind died down and it was completely calm.

He said to his disciples, "Why are you so afraid? Do you still have no faith?"

They were terrified and asked each other,

"Who is this? Even the wind and the waves obey him!"

The wind and the waves were not abnormal. Fierce winds, high waves, downpours—all were unexpected but not unusual. Until the end. The wind didn't slack and slowly die as the tail of the storm passed. Neither did the swells gradually retreat, losing their foam and froth until they merely lapped against the side of the boat. The storm simply quit—but not by itself. He told it to stop, to be still, and it was. In an instant. Smooth as glass.

It happened one day relatively early during Jesus's ministry of teaching and miracles. He was pressed by the crowds—understandable, given that He had been healing people of various sicknesses. They pressed Him tightly enough that He wanted to get into a boat and cross to the other side of the lake in order to breathe.

In the boat with His closest followers, some of whom had been career fishermen—used to the water and its ways, to say the least—an exhausted Jesus lay down in the stern and fell asleep. The group floated toward the other side, propelled by the wind and the oars. The trip was not more than ten miles, heading southeast from Capernaum. Their trip turned out to be a bit more exciting than they had anticipated.

Storms can form quickly on the water, especially when surrounded by mountains or hills. The mix of pressures and temperatures can change the atmospheric conditions quicky. "Getting set for a blow," mariners might say. The water isn't the most comfortable place to be when a storm starts to build. A three-hour tour can quickly become a harrowing rush for the shoreline.

It didn't look like they were going to make it to the shore. Feet were sloshing in water that had spilled into the bottom of the boat from the waves rolling over the gunwales. The only place the boat looked to be headed was the silty bottom.

There was water from above, water over the sides, and winds powerful enough to keep them from moving closer to the shore. The landlubbers on board were terrified. Even the seasoned fisherman were. When men like Peter and John began to show concern over their ability to make it through the storm—that's when panic set in.

Where was Jesus? Catching a quick nap in the stern.

Sleeping?! If there ever was a time for all hands on deck, this was it.

"Save us!" We're about to drown, and you're sleeping? Do something!

They may have been asking Him to help man the oars or pleading with Him for a miracle (probably the latter). They woke Jesus with a simple and desperate plea: "Lord, save us! We're going to drown!" (Matthew 8:25). This was a foxhole prayer, the request of someone certain that the end is near. *Jesus, look at what is happening. There is no way out unless you do something! Please! Do something!*

So Jesus did. He saved them all. Then He told them they had little faith and asked why they were so afraid. That's an odd question. True, they were safe now, but they had been about to sink.

Of course, they didn't. And the reason they didn't drown—the power behind their rescue—terrified them. As scared as they were of the storm, the sea, and what looked to be an inevitable and horrific death, Jesus did something that cracked their foundations. The unexpected storm was one-upped by the unexpected Jesus.

As though it were a petulant child, Jesus scolded the raging storm, told it to stop. And it did!

Life-threatening fear turned into existential terror as the now-safe seafarers wondered what kind of man commands the wind and the waves. A life-threatening boat ride in treacherous weather was not the scariest thing they came face-to-face with that night.

As fierce as the storm was, it's unlikely that the plea to be saved was a request to trim the mainsail or pull on an oar. They were asking for a miracle. And they got one. They got a miracle so big it scared them. A miracle so big they realized they really didn't know Jesus all that well.

"What kind of man is this?"

REFLECT

Jesus is certainly here with us, and the Holy Spirit lives in His followers, but we do not have Jesus's physical presence in our midst the way the disciples did. We don't have the same opportunity to be surprised by Him. We have the benefit of Scripture to help us understand Jesus. But sometimes what we think we know about Him may stop us from learning something new. When was the last time you were surprised by Jesus? Is it possible that how you think about Jesus can cause you to misunderstand Him (or yourself) from time to time?

Jesus, life can be scary. We often don't know what to do, what's happening around us, or what's coming next. Our circumstances can catch us by surprise, and before we know it, it can feel as if drowning is all but certain. It sometimes seems like You're asleep in the back of our boat.

Even though I know You are in my boat and I know that You can save, I am still afraid. It's not because I don't think You can save, but because it seems like You don't care. Thank You for being in my boat during my storm. [Name your storm here.] I know You can work outside of my expectations. Help me to be open to being surprised by the way You work. Amen.

17

THE GRATEFUL

Mark 5:14–20

Those tending the pigs ran off and reported this in the town and countryside, and the people went out to see what had happened. When they came to Jesus, they saw the man who had been possessed by the legion of demons, sitting there, dressed and in his right mind; and they were afraid. Those who had seen it told the people what had happened to the demon-possessed man—and told about the pigs as well. Then the people began to plead with Jesus to leave their region.

As Jesus was getting into the boat, the man who had been demon-possessed begged to go with him. Jesus did not let him, but said, "Go home to your own people and tell them how much the Lord has done for you, and how he has had mercy on you." So the man went away and began to tell in the Decapolis how much Jesus had done for him. And all the people were amazed.

When the people in the crowd came to themselves, they murmured to each other, trying to make sense of what their collective eyes were seeing: the madman, as he was less than affectionately known, was sitting in front of another man. He was clean, clothed, and listening calmly. There was little in his appearance to tie him to the naked, wild, strong man who used to howl among the tombs. So dramatic was the change that a number in the crowd doubted that it was actually him. But the swineherd's story, riveting from beginning to end, left little doubt.

The boat had landed, and a small band of men disembarked. As they settled the boat on the shore, a man came running from the tombs. He was wild in the most basic sense—naked, dirty, wide-eyed. Loud, unintelligible noise escaped his open mouth.

When he got to Jesus, he stopped and fell to his knees. The volume of his voice did not change, but the noises became words in response to Jesus's immediate command.

Jesus had seen the man was possessed by an evil spirit. Looking straight at the wild man, compassion and authority in His eyes and His voice, He commanded the demon to come out. The demon-possessed man's guttural shouts became an unsettling plea for mercy.

The power shift was shocking. The wild man's strength was nearly legendary. He had torn apart the chains and shackles used to bind him. He had cut himself with rocks while the demonic madness consumed him. He had dominated the area with his devilish insanity. He lived in solitary places and chased away any who dared to come near. Yet here he was, kneeling before Jesus and pleading for mercy. But it was not the man himself who was pleading.

Jesus spoke directly to the demon. But it was not just one, there were many. No wonder insanity seemed so close to the surface. Who could withstand the darkness of such an overwhelming presence?

Jesus had ordered the man's freedom, and the demons knew they must abandon their host. But they pleaded and groveled not to be tortured. They asked to be sent into the nearby herd of pigs. For reasons known only to Him, Jesus granted this request, and the horde of demons left the man and entered the pigs.

As if to validate the madness that had plagued the man while the swarm of demons infested him, the herd of swine immediately descended into their own madness. Snorting and squealing, they nearly trampled each other as they bolted down the hill and into the sea. Pigs don't swim. Their bloated carcasses washed up on shore for days.

The pig herders had seen enough. Much like their possessed, mad, and then drowned pigs, they fell over each other, running to town as fast as their feet would move.

One voice, then another, pleaded with Jesus to leave the area. Soon the entire crowd was urging Him away from their town. Some in the crowd were simply angry at the loss of the herd; they blamed Jesus for it. Others simply feared someone who possessed such power.

Jesus and His followers climbed back into the

boat. Whatever their reason for landing in the first place, the exorcism and subsequent loss of livestock and livelihood had cut their trip short.

The delivered man approached Jesus and begged to go with Him. He wanted to follow this man as closely as he could. Jesus had shown him mercy when he had known only rejection and torment. Jesus had shown His authority to a man who was subjugated to the whims of the spirits.

But Jesus would not let him come. "Go home to your own people and tell them how much the Lord has done for you, and how he has had mercy on you."

With that, the disciples shoved off and returned to the water. The freed man went home and, for the rest of his days, told the story of his deliverance, of Jesus's power and mercy.

REFLECT

The frightening familiar is often preferable to the terrifying unknown. When something changes and the reason for that change is mysterious, we can pine for what used to be, even if the new is objectively better. Have you ever been afraid of what Jesus might do next? Or what He might ask you to do?

Jesus has both the power and the mercy to bring deliverance to all who are in need. What part of your life is in need of His deliverance? Is there some part of your heart or mind you have banished to the lonely places because it cannot be controlled? How might you ask Jesus to have mercy on you? Do you let others know of all that God has done for you and of His mercy? If not, what is holding you back?

———

God of Freedom, You have done so much for us and shown us all great mercy. Thank You that You meet us where we are and offer us what only You can.

I confess I do not always respond by telling people what You have done for me. Forgive me for being silent about the mercy You have shown. Help me to spread the good news of what You have done for me. Amen.

18

THE BOLD

Mark 5:24–34

A large crowd followed and pressed around him. And a woman was there who had been subject to bleeding for twelve years. She had suffered a great deal under the care of many doctors and had spent all she had, yet instead of getting better she grew worse. When she heard about Jesus, she came up behind him in the crowd and touched his cloak, because she thought, "If I just touch his clothes, I will be healed." Immediately her bleeding stopped and she felt in her body that she was freed from her suffering.

At once Jesus realized that power had gone out from him. He turned around in the crowd and asked, "Who touched my clothes?"

"You see the people crowding against you,"

his disciples answered, "and yet you can ask, 'Who touched me?'"

But Jesus kept looking around to see who had done it. Then the woman, knowing what had happened to her, came and fell at his feet and, trembling with fear, told him the whole truth. He said to her, "Daughter, your faith has healed you. Go in peace and be freed from your suffering."

Twelve years of suffering trailed behind her. In front of her, hope, perhaps her only hope. If anyone in the crowd knew what her next hundred steps could mean for them, they would have stopped her far from her goal.

On what she hoped was the last day of her suffering, she remembered her first. The blood was of little concern, until it didn't stop. Curiosity grew into concern and then fear as days stretched into weeks and months.

Doctor after doctor saw her; still the bleeding continued. The physician's ministrations were often painful and never helpful. She held out hope, but as the years passed, she learned to live her life of uncleanness. Hers was a life of solitude, confined to her own unclean bed, alone in her unclean home. Unable to participate in her religion, to take part in the temple sacrifices and celebrations, or to meet with other people, she was cut off from the life she once knew.

Now, new hope walked through the crowd. Jesus, the man who had healed others—who had opened closed ears, illuminated blind eyes, strengthened weak, frail, and useless limbs, and reclaimed souls from malicious spirits—was nearly close enough to touch, and that was exactly her plan.

She was unknown here, so there was little chance she would be recognized and thwarted from her bold mission. Still, she knew she had to be discreet.

By turns she squeezed, tucked, and jostled deeper toward her target at the center of the crowd. She saw Him. He was tightly surrounded, guarded by an almost impenetrable wall of followers. Heaving and pulsing with the crowd, through the crowd, suddenly she was there, within arm's reach.

Desperation fed her boldness. She reached her arm between the two bodies in front of her; she stretched out for Him. Her fingers closed, empty, the moving crowd having shifted Him just beyond her grasp. She stumbled forward, trying to keep pace. She'd lost her spot close to the center.

Nearly wild with desperate anticipation, she threw caution to the wind, shoved people aside to regain proximity to her cure. She knew, she *knew* that just a touch would heal her. Even if only her fingers brushed His clothing, she would be healed.

He was there. She reached. A connection. The movement of Jesus in the crowd had billowed His cloak away from Him and just within reach of her stretched fingers. She could not grab, but she did not need to. Before her fingers lost connection with His cloak, she was healed. Four inches of fabric ended four thousand days of suffering. She felt the change. A tingle, small but deep, had flowed through her, salved her broken body, and set her free.

She stopped. Jesus stopped. The crowd stopped. Then the obvious came into her mind: *He knows. Jesus knows.* But of course He did. She had felt the power surge. He must have felt it too.

"Who touched my clothes?" Jesus scanned the crowd pressed in close around Him. The disciples' incredulous looks said enough. What a question!

Who didn't touch You? You see how many people are here and how anxious they are to be near You!

Jesus ignored their cynicism and continued studying the crowd. She knew He was looking for her. Eyes down, held breath straining in her lungs, she stepped out. She fell at His feet, joy and fear warring to master her emotions. She told Him. Everything. Twelve years of suffering and twelve minutes of action all tumbled out of her. She was sorry, but she needed to do what she did. She knew that touching Him would mend her broken body. And it had.

Jesus didn't have to say anything. His eyes of compassion told her enough. But He did speak, perhaps for the benefit of everyone else: "Daughter, your faith has healed you. Go in peace and be freed from your suffering." As Jesus sent her away, whole and healed, she knew it wasn't the end of her story; it was her new beginning.

REFLECT

Whether we know Him already or not, there are sometimes obstacles standing between us and Jesus. Is your faith strong enough that you push through the barriers to be close to Him? Are there struggles in your life that have been present for so long, you've given up on things ever changing? Is there a situation you're facing that has you stretching to touch Jesus's garment? Does your faith allow you to see past your lengthy struggle and push past the crowds to get to Jesus for help?

———————————

Jesus, thank You for reminding us that in our deepest moments of need, when it seems our hope vacated long ago, You are still there, within reach and able to heal us. Forgive us for letting the crowds stand in our way of reaching You. Grant us the faith we need to know You are with us and that we can reach out to You, whenever we draw near.

I confess that sometimes it is easier to stay in my struggles than it is to exert myself to find You. The long roads behind me and my many failed attempts to find healing have, perhaps, left me jaded and resigned. Give me the courage I need to step closer to You, no matter what stands in the way. Thank You for being compassionate and gracious. Amen.

19

THE HEARTBROKEN

Mark 5:35–43

While Jesus was still speaking, some people came from the house of Jairus, the synagogue leader. "Your daughter is dead," they said. "Why bother the teacher anymore?"

Overhearing what they said, Jesus told him, "Don't be afraid; just believe."

He did not let anyone follow him except Peter, James and John the brother of James. When they came to the home of the synagogue leader, Jesus saw a commotion, with people crying and wailing loudly. He went in and said to them, "Why all this commotion and wailing? The child is not dead but asleep." But they laughed at him.

After he put them all out, he took the child's father and mother and the disciples who were with him, and went in where the child was. He took her by the hand and said to her, "Talitha koum!" (which means "Little girl, I say to you, get up!"). Immediately the girl stood up and began to walk around (she was twelve years old). At this they were completely astonished. He gave strict orders not to let anyone know about this, and told them to give her something to eat.

The crowd had stopped and Jesus had spoken to a woman. Her story of suffering took only a minute to tell, and Jesus's words of healing, even less. But these words bolstered Jairus's confidence that Jesus could, and would, cure his daughter just as He had healed this other daughter of Abraham. His heart soared with renewed hope as he witnessed a display of the power and mercy he had come here for.

Jairus waited, as patiently as an anxious father could. He needed Jesus to finish so they could again be on their way. He felt a tug on his sleeve. Though this woman's grasp at Jesus's cloak brought her healing, this touch of his own cloak brought nothing of the kind.

He looked into the messenger's eyes. The

words hung in the air, their meaning turning hope into heartbreak. He had known that time could be short, but he had no idea it could be this short.

This intrusion had stolen moments from their journey, precious moments that may have kept his daughter alive long enough for Jesus to see her, touch her, heal her. This woman had taken the miracle that should have been his daughter's. Her twelve years of suffering was now over; his twelve-year-old daughter's life was too.

As he stared at the messenger, he felt another tug on his sleeve. "Don't be afraid. Just believe." It was Jesus. He looked into His eyes. He wanted to believe. He had just seen what belief could do. He would believe. How could he not believe?

Leaving the crowd behind, Jairus, Jesus, and a few of His followers continued on. Hope had resurrected in Jairus's heart. Jesus's word, and His presence beside him were restoring his expectations. But he was not prepared for the scene that confronted him.

He saw the mourners. Their presence was an announcement of tragedy, their wails tearing the air and assaulting his wounded heart. Jesus seemed unmoved, and when He spoke, the mood of the crowd shifted.

"Why all this commotion and wailing? The child is not dead but asleep." This fact was true for no one else but the Giver of life. The mourners' ignorance, as is often true of ignorance, erupted in laughter.

With an exasperated sigh, the paradoxically laughing mourners were ushered from the house. Then, Jairus's wife, oblivious to the events of her husband's trip, unaware of the words spoken to him about the need for faith, tugged at Jairus and whispered frantic questions. He had time only to relay Jesus's simple words, "Don't be afraid; just believe." Jesus ushered them, along with His three followers, into their little girl's room.

The sight nearly broke Jairus. His daughter lay on her bed. Jesus's words about her being asleep seemed almost mockingly true. If he hadn't heard the words from his own servant's mouth, seen and heard the mourners for himself, he would have thought she was merely sleeping. But there was no rise and fall to her chest, no soft whisper of inhale and exhale. Fear threatened to take him, to break him.

Jesus placed His hand on Jairus's shoulder as He walked forward to the girl's bed. The simple touch brought the words back, "Don't be afraid; just believe." Sheer force of will dragged his thoughts from the ridge of fear to what faith he could muster. Jesus said faith had healed the woman. Could it bring his daughter back? But faith in what, in who? Jesus? His healings were the reason Jairus had sought Him in the first place. Could Jesus bring his little girl back? Is that what He meant by "only sleeping"? Would He "wake" her?

Jesus looked at her for a long moment as He sat on her bed, the room unsettlingly quiet. No one but Jesus knew what was coming.

Leaning forward, Jesus gently called the girl to wake up. That whisper unleashed a torrent of life. The twelve-year-old girl virtually leapt from what was her death bed, her once-still body now overflowing with life.

Her mother and father nearly smothered her with their embrace. The disciples stood wide-eyed and speechless. Jesus, a smile of satisfaction lifting His lips, sat on the bed.

As He and His disciples left, His demeanor

changed slightly. Taking the family in with His gaze, He ordered them not to tell anyone about what happened. Then He softened and told Jairus to get his daughter something to eat. With those words, He left the family to their joy.

REFLECT

Fear can cripple us, make us say and do things we never would under other circumstances. It provokes us to fight or flee. What situations, real or possible, cause a fearful response to rise up within you? How do you respond to that fear? Jesus told Jairus to have faith rather than give in to his fear, even though the object of that fear—the death of his daughter—was a present reality. What might it look like for you to exercise faith in a situation that causes you fear? What can you do to act in faith rather than respond in fear?

Giver of Life, there are many things in this world that make us afraid. We are often consumed by thoughts of all that can go wrong, worried about an unexpected moment that can change things forever. Sometimes that fear leads us to lash out or curl up and hide.

Forgive me for the times I've let fear control my actions. Forgive me for giving in to the anxiety of the unknown. Help me to hear Your call not to be afraid but to have faith. Even though You may not "raise my daughter" as you did for Jairus, I know You are the Lord of life and are with me and for me. Help me to rest in Your perfect love. Grant me the strength to bring my darkest fears into the light of Your presence. Amen.

20

THE
SKEPTICAL

Mark 6:1–6

Jesus left there and went to his hometown, accompanied by his disciples. When the Sabbath came, he began to teach in the synagogue, and many who heard him were amazed.

"Where did this man get these things?" they asked. "What's this wisdom that has been given him? What are these remarkable miracles he is performing? Isn't this the carpenter? Isn't this Mary's son and the brother of James, Joseph, Judas and Simon? Aren't his sisters here with us?" And they took offense at him.

Jesus said to them, "A prophet is not without honor except in his own town, among his relatives and in his own home." He could not do any miracles there, except lay his hands on a few sick people and heal them. He was amazed at their lack of faith.

After He started traveling the countryside, preaching and performing miracles, Jesus returned to speak at His home synagogue. He went home to share with those He had known the longest, with those who knew Him best. But things had certainly changed since He was last home. Jesus was now a traveling teacher and miracle worker.

Murmurs of conversation faded as Jesus began to speak. His words floated over the audience; the people sat transfixed. His words were captivating, the message unlike anything they'd heard.

The murmurs started again. Neighbors leaned to each other and commented. There were excited whispers repeating the memorable phrases and ideas. Like a breeze that forces a deep breath, Jesus's words squeezed into the cracks of hearts and minds.

A surprise was the last thing anyone expected that day. But this was fantastic! This was the kind of message that pushed you out the door and made you want to do something new, different, bigger, better. Who would've thought *this guy* was going to do this? Everyone knew Him. He grew up down the road. He helped His dad fix our table. He played with our kids in the backyard.

Wait—this was wrong. It all sounded nice, but the more Jesus spoke, the more the murmurs turned to sarcasm and questions. It was true; the message was brilliant, the delivery engaging. But this, this was Jesus! The down-home perception of Him began to reassert itself in the minds of His listeners. Skeptical questions began to roll unfiltered from their lips: "Where did this man get these things?" they asked. "What's this wisdom that has been given him? What are these remarkable miracles He's performing? Isn't this the carpenter? Isn't this Mary's son and the brother of James, Joseph, Judas and Simon? Aren't his sisters here with us?"

They were offended. "We know Jesus!" they whispered to one another. "Who does He think He is?"

They were indeed astonished at His wisdom. They wondered at the powerful miracles. But when they thought about Him and who He was, they kept Him in the place they had always known

Him. In fact, there is one question that crystalizes their view of Him: "Isn't this the carpenter?"

They asked the question in the present tense. They did not ask, "*Wasn't* He a carpenter?" They asked, "*Isn't* He the carpenter?" His hometown friends were stuck on Jesus as they knew Him. He was gone long enough to become someone of significant reputation, but not long enough for people to allow Him to become someone other than who they knew.

Amazement turned to ridicule as the people of Nazareth pushed Jesus back into the hole they had for Him. Whatever excitement Jesus had at His homecoming quickly became incredulous amazement at the unbelief of His friends and family. That unbelief restricted what Jesus was able to do. He could not do any miracles there *because of* their unbelief.

Jesus's hometown friends missed out on what Jesus had been doing in the other towns and villages He visited—the preaching, the teaching, and the miracles. They knew He was saying incredible things in His teaching. They had heard He was performing miracles of healing. But they did not believe. They did not believe He could be anything other than the Jesus they had known as a carpenter. They didn't believe He could be all that different than His brothers and sisters or anyone else in town. And because they couldn't let Him out of that box, they missed what He could have given them. "He could not do any miracles there."

Pigeonholing Jesus doesn't take away His power. The unbelief of the people of Nazareth didn't make Him any less the Messiah, so why didn't He heal people and restore sight to the blind? Because He never got the opportunity. He wasn't allowed to perform any miracles. The blind, deaf, dumb, sick, paralyzed, and possessed were not brought to Him in His hometown as they were in other places (although He did heal a few sick people). The throngs of people following Him through the countryside were replaced with eye rolls and closed doors. The life and strength He could have given remained unfulfilled desires. Pigeonholed unbelief is us closing the door on Jesus.

REFLECT

Pigeonholing, stereotyping, prejudging. They all wrap themselves around our relationships and squeeze them. Many of the people in Jesus's day missed recognizing Him, because they knew what Messiah was supposed to do. Not only did Jesus not do the things they thought He was supposed to do, He did things they weren't prepared to accept the Messiah was going to do.

The closer we get to Jesus, the better we'll know Him (like those who grew up with Him) and the more prone we may be to think we've got Him all figured out. How open are you to Jesus working in unexpected and uncomfortable ways? What if the Lord is moving in an unexpected way and you, in your certainty, are missing it?

Jesus, we are creatures of habit. We don't adjust easily to change, especially when it's unexpected. We would rather stick with what we're used to. The mundane and predictable is an easier path to walk. We tend to keep people "in their place" because it is less dangerous for us when we know who someone is and what to expect from them. But that isn't fair to them, and it doesn't make room for the work You may be doing in their life.

You have changed me, and I want people to know it. I want to be open to the good You would have me do. I also want to be open to the good You are doing in the world, even if it's not how I would expect or in ways I can easily understand. Help me to see with Your eyes the work You are doing in the world around me. Forgive me for being skeptical. Help me to see growth in others, just as I want others to see the growth in me. Amen.

21

THE WILLING

Mark 6:31–44

Then, because so many people were coming and going that they did not even have a chance to eat, he said to them, "Come with me by yourselves to a quiet place and get some rest."

So they went away by themselves in a boat to a solitary place. But many who saw them leaving recognized them and ran on foot from all the towns and got there ahead of them. When Jesus landed and saw a large crowd, he had compassion on them, because they were like sheep without a shepherd. So he began teaching them many things.

By this time it was late in the day, so his disciples came to him. "This is a remote place," they said, "and it's already very late. Send the people away so that they can go to the surrounding countryside and villages and buy themselves something to eat."

But he answered, "You give them something to eat."

They said to him, "That would take more than half a year's wages! Are we to go and spend that much on bread and give it to them to eat?"

"How many loaves do you have?" he asked. "Go and see."

When they found out, they said, "Five—and two fish."

Then Jesus directed them to have all the people sit down in groups on the green grass. So they sat down in groups of hundreds and fifties. Taking the five loaves and the two fish and looking up to heaven, he gave thanks and broke the loaves. Then he gave them to his disciples to distribute to the people. He also divided the two fish among them all. They all ate and were satisfied, and the disciples picked up twelve basketfuls of broken pieces of bread and fish. The number of the men who had eaten was five thousand.

It was finally catching up to them. The excitement drove them relentlessly on, frequently, but temporarily, dispelling their weariness. Now the disciples were exhausted. The pace of the movement had stretched them to their limit. They needed rest—time alone, time away from the crowds, time to think, to understand.

So Jesus invited them into the boat, to come away with Him and rest. But Jesus could not hide. His presence and location were impossible to conceal. The crowds wanted to be around Jesus, to hear His words and receive His miracles. They saw Him get into the boat, saw where He was headed and rushed to meet Him there. A multitude awaited Him on the shore when they landed.

As the boat took the shore, Jesus's heart went out to the crowd. They needed guidance; they had been so long not knowing how to follow God. They did not truly understand what it meant to be His people.

Jesus began to teach them. His words captivated them until the sun had finished tracing its arc across the sky. As the hours grew late, the disciples looked out at the crowd. The compassion of Jesus taking root in their own hearts, they were concerned about the people. Where and how would all of these people find something to eat? They did what they could about their concern; they took the problem to Jesus.

Jesus, gratified by His disciples' care and concern for the crowd, did what He often did. He gave an unexpected response: "You give them something to eat." Seeing the problem was only the first step; true compassion required doing something about it.

They had come here on the boat together. Jesus knew they did not travel with food. They often needed to go into nearby villages to buy food for themselves. He knew their funds as well. They lived on the donations and support of others. The cost of even a snack for everyone in a crowd this size would stretch to nearly half a year's wages. But Jesus, undeterred by the disciples' impossible hurdle, simply asked how much bread they had.

Not much. They returned with five loaves and two small fish, the meager meal of a small boy. It was laughably not enough. But Jesus had asked for what they had, and they gave it to Him.

The cluster of discussion between Jesus and His disciples, and the small amount of food the crowd saw had them guessing about what was happening. The disciples divided the crowd into groups and had them sit on the ground. Everyone watched Jesus.

He prayed a simple blessing over the loaves and began to break them and pass them out. As the people watched the five loaves and two fish get distributed to the disciples, some remembered the stories of Elisha—how he had multiplied olive oil on one occasion and bread on another. Each disciple took some bread and fish and began to pass it to the groups. Everyone took some, being careful not to take too much, and passed it. They all ate. And they all ate more. They all ate until they were full.

No one saw anything happen to the bread. Somehow it was enough. Jesus had taken what was given and did what only He could do; He made what was offered enough to accomplish what He had asked.

REFLECT

Sometimes Jesus asks us for more than we have. We feel Him calling us to something we know we cannot accomplish. It's not that we just don't feel ready or we don't want to do what He's asking. Rather, we simply do not have the resources. When Jesus asks, do you offer Him what you have? What you have in time, money, prayer, faith, skill? When Jesus asks, "I can't" is not an acceptable reply. What is Jesus asking you to do? What are the reasons you are or are not acting on what He has asked?

Jesus, Lord of the harvest, You have chosen to do Your work in and through us. You ask us to work with You to accomplish the advancement of Your kingdom until You return. Thank You for trusting us to carry Your gospel.

Sometimes it seems like the work is too much. I may be tired or simply not have the needed resources. Help me to be honest with You about what I have. Remind me that my lack is not an excuse to withhold what I do have. Forgive me for the excuses I make and my wrong priorities. Thank You for multiplying my meager offerings to accomplish Your purposes. Amen.

22

THE
COURAGEOUS

Matthew 14:22–33

Immediately Jesus made the disciples get into the boat and go on ahead of him to the other side, while he dismissed the crowd. After he had dismissed them, he went up on a mountainside by himself to pray. Later that night, he was there alone, and the boat was already a considerable distance from land, buffeted by the waves because the wind was against it.

Shortly before dawn Jesus went out to them, walking on the lake. When the disciples saw him walking on the lake, they were terrified. "It's a ghost," they said, and cried out in fear.

But Jesus immediately said to them: "Take courage! It is I. Don't be afraid."

"Lord, if it's you," Peter replied, "tell me to come to you on the water."

"Come," he said.

Then Peter got down out of the boat, walked on the water and came toward Jesus. But when he saw the wind, he was afraid and, beginning to sink, cried out, "Lord, save me!"

Immediately Jesus reached out his hand and caught him. "You of little faith," he said, "why did you doubt?"

And when they climbed into the boat, the wind died down. Then those who were in the boat worshiped him, saying, "Truly you are the Son of God."

It was just the twelve of them now. They weren't all seamen, but enough of them were to manage the vessel safely to the other side of the lake. The wind had picked up; few in the boat seemed to mind. The cresting waters made the going slow, but old muscles remembered their cadence at the oars, and minds were free to wander over the events of the day.

John the baptizer was dead, martyred by a spiteful woman and a rash ruler. Jesus had taken them away after that news. They needed time to eat, to rest, to mourn and comfort one another. But Jesus couldn't hide. Even in desolate places, the people found Him.

Perhaps He saw His desire for comfort mirrored in the people who came to Him. Carrying their sick and broken, they looked lost—so many sheep without a shepherd. Grief, as so often happens, gave rise to compassion. In that lonely place where Jesus and His disciples intended to find comfort for their own weariness and grief, Jesus offered it to others. His hands touched broken bodies and made them whole. His words quickened broken hearts and minds.

Hunger rose as the sun sank. It was late, and they were far from provisions. If the miraculous healings hadn't been enough, Jesus took a child's lunch, a mere snack for any grown man, and fed the crowd, every last soul.

Then Jesus found His solitude. Sending the disciples back across the water, He found a quiet place to pray.

In the small hours of the night, when the darkness is deep, they were still at the oars. The wind was still thwarting their progress, their muscles and minds weary from the strain of a long night. Then they saw it—a figure coming toward them on top of the water.

Terror held them as the seeming apparition closed the distance. Minds and bodies paralyzed with fear refused to respond as the figure continued coming toward them. "It's a ghost!"

A familiar voice floated across the water, "Take courage! It is I. Don't be afraid."

It was the Lord coming to his friends after His own long night. Taking the direct route to His followers, He approached them on the water. But the disciples, accustomed to miracles though they may have been, could not place the figure moving on the water as their Lord. Distance, fatigue, the nature of this unique miracle, or maybe all three clouded their recognition of the man they followed, until He spoke.

Peter, perhaps eager to prove it was Jesus, and perhaps to prove himself, called back. "If it is you, tell me to come to you on the water." Peter knew that if the ghostly figure was indeed the Lord, he had the power to allow Peter to walk on the water. The request was Peter's. His was the fear. His was the desire for proof, and the plan. His was the courage to ask, for if called, it would be his feet on the waves.

Jesus called. Peter had the desire. Jesus had the power.

The weariness of his arms and back forgotten, Peter flexed his faith, grabbed the gunwale and looked at the lapping waves. Then he stepped out. Under his feet, the waters were as firm as the shore. Fear faded to wonder as he gazed at his Lord and walked to meet Him.

But the water didn't flatten, and the wind still howled. Peter was not walking on a sea of glass; he was walking through the wind-driven crests of a dangerous sea. Despite the number of steps he'd already taken, his boldness began to sink, and so did he. Peter did not have the faith to carry out his own request.

Peter had asked Jesus for something, and Jesus had granted the request. Peter did not ask for the wind and the waves to calm. He asked to meet Jesus in the wind and waves, and it was those very waves on which he first stood that capsized his confidence in the power of Jesus.

Jesus didn't call Peter to step out of the boat. He was coming to them in the boat. It was Peter who asked to come to Jesus. And it was only when Peter's faith failed in the middle of the task *he asked to accomplish* that Jesus evaluated Peter's faith. Once the request was made and the permission given, Jesus expected Peter to walk to Him on the waves.

REFLECT

We know that God has the power to do the incredible. The stories of His acts in history and in our own lives testify to His power and goodness. How often do you ask Him for something that seems impossible? Peter asked to do something special, something Jesus had not called him to do. Jesus granted his request and expected Peter to carry out his part. What have you asked Jesus for? Are you willing to walk in faith when He answers yes?

Jesus, thank You for coming to us in the wind and waves of our lives. Thank You for being with us and for us when life is difficult and when the sea that surrounds us threatens our progress. We know You have the power to both calm the seas and to allow us to walk on them.

Help me to know You are there when I am afraid. I confess that sometimes my faith falters even in the midst of answered prayers. Help me to keep my eyes on You as the wind blows around me and the waves lap at my feet. Amen.

23

THE
HARD-HEARTED

Mark 6:45–52

Immediately Jesus made his disciples get into the boat and go on ahead of him to Bethsaida, while he dismissed the crowd. After leaving them, he went up on a mountainside to pray.

Later that night, the boat was in the middle of the lake, and he was alone on land. He saw the disciples straining at the oars, because the wind was against them. Shortly before dawn he went out to them, walking on the lake. He was about to pass by them, but when they saw him walking on the lake, they thought he was a ghost. They cried out, because they all saw him and were terrified.

Immediately he spoke to them and said, "Take courage! It is I. Don't be afraid." Then he climbed into the boat with them, and the wind died down. They were completely amazed, for they had not understood about the loaves; their hearts were hardened.

It had the feel of an escape, absconding with a feast of leftovers. Each of the disciples with a basketful of bread and fish climbed into the boat and went ahead of Jesus, who would meet them in Bethsaida after He dismissed the crowd.

The disciples hadn't had time to think about what had happened on the mountainside. Now, as the oars fell into their familiar rhythm, pulling at the chop beneath the boat, their minds were free to wander. And from the feel of the wind, there was going to be plenty of time to think.

As it was with earlier miracles, those who saw it were in awe, including the disciples. Clearly the power of God was at work in Jesus. Few thought otherwise. But Israel's history contained plenty of miracle workers. Though now well beyond the memory of even the eldest in the land, the stories were not gone. And now, it seemed, there was a new messenger from God.

Those who witnessed Jesus's miracles went

away praising God. Many were changed forever by their encounter with Jesus. But the miracles were never an end in themselves; they revealed the heart of the Father and confirmed Jesus's own teaching about Himself and God's kingdom.

Men, women, and children had all been filled that day, their hearts with new teaching and wisdom, and their stomachs with the miraculous meal from a generous little boy's lunch. Unfortunately, that was all they left with. The deeper meaning of Jesus's identity—that God had come to His people—eluded all of them, including the disciples.

Back on the shore, Jesus had sent the spiritually and physically fed crowd to their homes. Alone, He ascended the mountain to spend time praying.

Hours passed. Jesus looked over the lake and saw His friends struggling at the oars, the wind and waves robbing their strokes of strength. They were in no peril, but they were tired. Their minds and bodies were spent. They had set out to find some quiet rest, instead they found more work— spending their little energy on the crowds and at work on the sea.

Jesus went to His friends. The wind offered no

resistance, and the waves offered solid footing beneath Him as He, in clear manifestation of His deity, walked on the water toward the boat.

The disciples squinted in the darkness as something became visible out on the water. Hands rubbed eyes that wearily blinked away the tiredness. Minds that had been wandering snapped to attention, trying to make sense of what the eyes were taking in.

But weary minds and bodies do not always reach the right conclusions, and a figure on the water in the middle of the night is not easily comprehended. What could have been a revelation and a comfort was instead terrifying. There, barely visible through the darkness, in the deepest part of the sea, was the figure of a man, strolling alongside the boat.

Fear leapt from man to man, and the boat listed hard as the disciples crowded one another to get as far as they could from the ghost on the water. The feelings of warmth brought by the day's teaching and miracle were chilled by the rising dread brought by the apparent specter. The monotony of the night's rowing was forgotten in a moment as each disciple's mind raced.

The figure spoke.

The words floated to them and, as sound on the water does, drew the figure even closer. But that closeness was welcome as the meaning of the words settled on them, calmed their minds, and extinguished their terror.

"Take courage! It is I. Do not be afraid." It was the Master. Jesus had come to them, strolling confidently through the wind and on the water that had opposed the disciples all night. He climbed into the boat with them, and as He did, the wind slackened, and the waves flattened. The night calmed. But the disciples' minds did not.

Reflection and monotony had become terror as an unknown and unexpected figure approached them on the water. That fear was relieved by the sound of Jesus's voice, but quickly became wonder as His very presence in the boat brought peace to them, and to the wind and waves that had battered them all night.

REFLECT

The disciples did not recognize Jesus. Just as they couldn't make out His appearance when He was walking to them on the water, they hadn't understood His full identity when He multiplied fish and loaves. They failed to understand that in that miracle, they were seeing not just the power and care of God, but the very presence of God in the face of Jesus. Are there times when you fail to recognize Jesus? What's keeping you from seeing and understanding who Jesus is and what He is doing in your life?

Provider God, thank You for revealing Yourself and Your love for us in the life and miracles of Jesus.

Help me to see where You are working and what You are doing. Help me to see where my heart may be hard and how that stops me from recognizing You. I confess that sometimes I am so wrapped up in my own life that I am startled—even scared—by that which should bring me comfort. Thank You for coming to me and showing me who You are. Thank You for always taking care of me. Amen.

24

THE DESPAIRING

Mark 7:24–30

Jesus left that place and went to the vicinity of Tyre. He entered a house and did not want anyone to know it; yet he could not keep his presence secret. In fact, as soon as she heard about him, a woman whose little daughter was possessed by an impure spirit came and fell at his feet. The woman was a Greek, born in Syrian Phoenicia. She begged Jesus to drive the demon out of her daughter.

"First let the children eat all they want," he told her, "for it is not right to take the children's bread and toss it to the dogs."

"Lord," she replied, "even the dogs under the table eat the children's crumbs."

Then he told her, "For such a reply, you may go; the demon has left your daughter."

She went home and found her child lying on the bed, and the demon gone.

The still of her daughter's sleep brought deep relief and revealed, by contrast, how difficult the days had been. She stroked her daughter's hair. Sleep now seemed the only respite for either of them. In waking hours, the demon's torment was constant. It gave the little girl no peace and kept her mother busy intervening in her daughter's demonically instigated destruction.

She was at the end of herself. There were no doctors or medicines that could cure her daughter. Her prayers and offerings at the temple of Melqart had changed nothing. She had even taken her daughter to the temple so that the god could see her daughter and perhaps take pity on them. Still her daughter remained possessed.

She didn't know how to expel the demon from her daughter. She didn't understand why it had come in the first place. She knew she needed a miracle. If something did not change soon, she was going to lose her daughter; no one could sustain the demonic torture.

She had heard of a man who could be just what

her daughter needed. His name was Jesus, and He was a Jew. Word had reached Tyre that He was a miracle worker. He healed diseases, raised the dead, and even cast out demons. Would He be able to help? But He was Jewish and in Israel. She could not leave her daughter behind to travel to find Him, and she could not take her daughter to Him.

Despair smothered her; help for her daughter was just out of reach. She sat in the quietness of her daughter's room and wept, her own helplessness drawing heavy sobs from deep in her chest. She had to find a way to help her daughter.

The ongoing rumors and reports about Jesus added deeper levels of frustration and despair to her plight. With each new story, she grew more convinced that Jesus could help her daughter.

And then an impossible rumor reached her. Jesus, the miracle worker and exorcist, was here. He was in Tyre! Now was her time. She would find Him and convince Him to rescue her daughter.

Quick questions revealed exactly where Jesus was staying. Her despair drove her through the city to the door of the house that held her miracle. There was no hesitation; there was not time to be timid. She went inside.

He was not hard to identify. He was the only Jew in the room. She threw herself at His feet. "Please, Jesus, my daughter has a demon. Please drive it out."

"First let the children eat all they want," he told her, "for it is not right to take the children's bread and toss it to the dogs."

No? She would not settle for that. This was her daughter. Yes, she was Greek. Yes, she understood that Jesus was saying His power and miracles were for the Jews. But wasn't there something He could do? Surely His presence in her city meant something!

"Lord," she replied, "even the dogs under the table eat the children's crumbs."

Is there nothing You can spare for those others who are in need? Surely the goodness and mercy being shown to Israel can spill over, even just a little, to help the rest of the world.

Then He told her, "For such a reply, you may go; the demon has left your daughter."

Relief flooded through her. She did not doubt. She trusted the words this man spoke were true, that the demon had indeed left her daughter. Her thank-you was quick but sincere as she fled through the door and back to her home, back to her daughter.

There she was, standing in the doorway, eyes clear and bright with a smile on her face and recognition in her eyes. Mother and daughter embraced as though they had not seen each other in months. In some ways, they had not. This was a reunion, a moment of deep joy that rivaled the depth of her despair.

REFLECT

Moments of despair can drive us to take uncharacteristic action. The woman in today's story was likely in the grip of a deep despair over the condition of her daughter. She went to Jesus in hope, looking for mercy, and she received it. Do you have situations in your life that leave you in despair? How might you pray differently, asking Jesus to intervene in that situation? What would it mean to continue to pursue Jesus even after there has been an answer to your request? What does persistence in prayer mean for you?

Jesus, thank You for showing us Your goodness and Your power. Thank You for having mercy on us when we need mercy.

Help me to remember that there is no darkness that cannot be dispelled by Your light and that, though the road may be longer than I want, You are there with me and working for me in my circumstances, even when I do not see or understand how. Thank You for not leaving me in my despair, but for bringing me into the hope and light of Your kingdom. Amen.

25

THE INSPIRED

Matthew 16:13–20

When Jesus came to the region of Caesarea Philippi, he asked his disciples, "Who do people say the Son of Man is?"

They replied, "Some say John the Baptist; others say Elijah; and still others, Jeremiah or one of the prophets."

"But what about you?" he asked. "Who do you say I am?"

Simon Peter answered, "You are the Messiah, the Son of the living God."

Jesus replied, "Blessed are you, Simon son of Jonah, for this was not revealed to you by flesh and blood, but by my Father in heaven. And I tell you that you are Peter, and on this rock I will build my church, and the gates of Hades

will not overcome it. I will give you the keys of
the kingdom of heaven; whatever you bind on
earth will be bound in heaven, and whatever
you loose on earth will be loosed in heaven."
Then he ordered his disciples not to tell anyone
that he was the Messiah.

Leaving the crowds behind, the leader takes
His group to a place far away from the ears
and eyes of the curious, the excited, and the
skeptical. Stopping, He turns to face His trusted
friends.

Here it's safe. It's private. It's the right place
to have a serious and necessary conversation.
And He poses a question: "Who do people say
that I am?"

It's a setup for a follow-up question, and the
answer will reveal the effect of the last several
years. Years of speaking, of miracles, of touching
hearts, minds, and bodies. What are the people
saying about Jesus?

The answers offered are varied—almost hu-
morous.

"John the Baptist!"

"Elijah!"

"Jeremiah or one of the prophets!"

These were mostly logical speculations. Each answer has something fundamentally similar. Each of these individuals called the Jewish people back to faithfulness to God. But each answer also suggests something about those who offered it.

John the Baptist. This appears to be the uninformed response of the uninterested. While the ministries of Jesus and John the Baptist had similarities, it would be impossible for the two to be the same man. They both preached at the same time. They had even stood together in the river as John baptized Jesus. The suggestion that Jesus is John seems to indicate that the responder knew *someone* was doing *something* but didn't necessarily care to sort it all out.

Elijah. This is a more informed response. The people who thought this likely knew Elijah's significance in Israelite history. Elijah was expected to return to minister to the people of Israel before the day of the Lord, a time that included the coming of the Messiah. These people were religiously interested and informed; they were looking for something from God. They were wrong, but they were headed in the right direction.

Jeremiah or one of the prophets. This may be the response of the traditionalists and culturalists. The people of Israel had a long history of prophets speaking to them. Almost since the beginning of the nation, prophets had been a part of the Israelite experience. It's possible that those who referred to Jesus as such were simply suggesting He was just another in a long line of prophets, as if to say, "This is the status quo for us as a people and, hence, not really all that unusual."

Jesus asked His disciples how the winds of opinion about Him were blowing through the towns and villages. His response wasn't surprise or disappointment; it almost seems He expected this mosaic of His identity. Not satisfied with what was being said "out there," Jesus turned the question on His handpicked followers: "Who do you say I am?"

Peter was the first to respond: "You are the Messiah, the Son of the living God." Did they all believe this? It's possible that Peter was speaking for the group, that they had had this discussion among themselves. Or perhaps this was just Peter's idea. Regardless, Jesus declared this an inspired response, revealed by His Father in heaven. Revealed how? That's impossible for us to say with absolute certainty. What's important is that Jesus affirmed the answer as the truth. He was indeed the Messiah.

Jesus wanted to know what people thought of Him not because His self-perception and self-worth rested on the opinions of others, but because His life and mission presented a question that needed to be answered.

People responded to Jesus in a variety of ways. They came as seekers and skeptics, as people in need of rescue and people struggling with confusion. Some came with antagonism while others came with honest curiosity. People still approach Jesus from these vantage points today, because the question Jesus asked His disciples is still necessary. "Who do you say I am?" The question filters its way through time and culture to present itself to everyone, and everyone has to answer sometime.

Who do you say Jesus is?

REFLECT

Responding to Jesus is not a one-time event. The disciples' journey with Jesus in the flesh demonstrates this. They were regularly faced with circumstances that made them rethink who Jesus was and how they were going to respond to Him. We may have settled the question of who Jesus is, but we, like them, are constantly faced with the question of how we will respond to Him. Even if we've previously responded to Him in faith, new circumstances in life will demand we respond to Him again.

Have you always responded the same way to Jesus?

Do you remember any times when you had to choose how you would respond to Jesus?

Have you ever responded differently? Under what circumstances has your response changed?

Jesus, we know all too well that our response to You can change. Even though we desire to stay true to You, there are times when we still wrestle with how we should respond to You. We may be confused, curious, in need of rescue, even skeptical. Thank You for always coming back to us and asking us to trust You anew, for giving us another chance to respond to You.

You are the Messiah, the Son of the living God. At times, I have let the circumstances of life push me to react to You in ways that do not match my love for You. I have been unfaithful to You in so many ways. Help me not to think in once-and-for-all terms, but to take each moment of life as it comes. As each one does, help me to respond to You this one time. Help me to accept Your mission and to carry it out as I travel through my life's journey. Amen.

26

THE DESPERATE

Mark 9:14–27

When they came to the other disciples, they saw a large crowd around them and the teachers of the law arguing with them. As soon as all the people saw Jesus, they were overwhelmed with wonder and ran to greet him.

"What are you arguing with them about?" he asked.

A man in the crowd answered, "Teacher, I brought you my son, who is possessed by a spirit that has robbed him of speech. Whenever it seizes him, it throws him to the ground. He foams at the mouth, gnashes his teeth and becomes rigid. I asked your disciples to drive out the spirit, but they could not."

"You unbelieving generation," Jesus replied,

"how long shall I stay with you? How long shall I put up with you? Bring the boy to me."

So they brought him. When the spirit saw Jesus, it immediately threw the boy into a convulsion. He fell to the ground and rolled around, foaming at the mouth.

Jesus asked the boy's father, "How long has he been like this?"

"From childhood," he answered. "It has often thrown him into fire or water to kill him. But if you can do anything, take pity on us and help us."

"'If you can'?" said Jesus. "Everything is possible for one who believes."

Immediately the boy's father exclaimed, "I do believe; help me overcome my unbelief!"

When Jesus saw that a crowd was running to the scene, he rebuked the impure spirit. "You deaf and mute spirit," he said, "I command you, come out of him and never enter him again."

The spirit shrieked, convulsed him violently and came out. The boy looked so much like a corpse that many said, "He's dead." But Jesus took him by the hand and lifted him to his feet, and he stood up.

The three men walking down the mountain with Jesus shared a glance. Jesus's instruction not to tell the others about what had happened on the mountain was, perhaps, not needed. What they had witnessed boggled the mind.

But there was little time for reflection. The low rumble of tense voices from the foot of the mountain reached them well before they arrived at the bottom. As one, the crowd surged and enveloped the newcomers. Unfortunately, the arrival of Jesus did not ease the tensions.

He asked, "What are you arguing about?"

A thin, desperate voice rose from the crowd. "This is about my son." Like many before him, he had brought a suffering loved one to Jesus to be healed.

The father had related his son's plight to the disciples, just as he had rehearsed it. His son was demon possessed. The demon had taken away the boy's ability to speak. On occasion, it would give him seizures during which he would fall to the ground and become rigid, foaming at the mouth and gnashing his teeth.

The disciples looked at the poor boy with pity

while they listened to the father's tale. Memories of exorcisms and healings they had witnessed on their own recent travels played through their minds. They comforted the father and offered to help, reassuring him they could cast out demons. Relief overwhelmed the grateful man, and he placed his son in front of the disciples.

But relief was quickly swallowed by despair. The demon remained. The disciples had failed.

That was when Jesus appeared. The father stepped forward from the crowd and stood in front of Jesus. He told how the disciples were unable to release his son from the grip of the demon.

Tense silence draped over the crowd as Jesus looked out, His eyes resting a moment on the teachers of the law and His own disciples. His words were directed at everyone and at no one in particular, "You unbelieving generation, how long shall I stay with you? How long shall I put up with you? Bring the boy to me."

The father stared, unsure how the statements hung together. The criticism was clear, but who was guilty? This man had brought his child, knowing that Jesus had healed others, believing that Jesus could also help his son.

The disciples, still near the boy, picked him up and brought him to Jesus. But as soon as the spirit recognized Jesus, it staked its claim on the boy, showing the power it had over him. Years of seizures had not dulled their effect on the father. He rushed to his son's side, attempting to restrain and comfort until the episode passed.

Jesus just watched. "How long has he been like this?"

Holding his son, the father replied, "Since childhood. It has tried to kill him in fire and water." The disappointment of the disciples' failure still fresh, he pleaded, "If you can do anything, take pity on us and help us."

Jesus's reply revealed that the father was indeed part of the unbelieving generation. If he would only believe, it would be possible. The revelation tore at the father's heart. His disbelief was a barrier to his son's release. "Please, help my unbelief," he begged.

Jesus commanded the spirit to leave. In a final act of rebellion, the spirit shook the boy violently. Then it shrieked and left him.

No one spoke. Everyone strained to see the boy, limp, pale, and motionless in his father's arms, his open eyes staring vacantly into the sky. To all who could see, it seemed the spirit finally killed him as it left.

Jesus reached down and took the boy's small hand. His eyes regained their focus, his head lifted, and holding Jesus's hand, he stood up. There were no more words. The father's belief rose with the boy and found focus on the man holding his son's hand.

REFLECT

Sometimes it seems that Jesus wants to talk before He acts. There were many points at which Jesus could have removed the demon, but He did not. Even when the demon was in full possession of the boy, He did not immediately act. Certainly, the father could be excused for being impatient, but Jesus's timing is His own. How has Jesus's timing had an impact on your faith? What desperate situations do you face in which you need what only Jesus can provide? Does your past experience bolster or detract from your belief that Jesus can provide?

Jesus, we are desperate for what only You can provide. Salvation, mercy, healing, help. Our desperation can take many forms. Help us to seek You and bring our trials to You. We know Your timing is not always what we want, but a delay in response does not indicate an absence of presence, power, or care.

I confess that sometimes my faith is small and I do not know it. Help me in my unbelief. Help me to know what it is to trust You with all of my life. Give me the strength to give You what I hold most dear. Give me the faith to trust You are able to provide what I need, no matter how desperate I become. Amen.

27

THE CONDEMNED

John 8:2–11

At dawn he appeared again in the temple courts, where all the people gathered around him, and he sat down to teach them. The teachers of the law and the Pharisees brought in a woman caught in adultery. They made her stand before the group and said to Jesus, "Teacher, this woman was caught in the act of adultery. In the Law Moses commanded us to stone such women. Now what do you say?" They were using this question as a trap, in order to have a basis for accusing him.

But Jesus bent down and started to write on the ground with his finger. When they kept on questioning him, he straightened up and said to them, "Let any one of you who is without sin be the first to throw a stone at her." Again he stooped down and wrote on the ground.

At this, those who heard began to go away one at a time, the older ones first, until only Jesus was left, with the woman still standing there. Jesus straightened up and asked her, "Woman, where are they? Has no one condemned you?"

"No one, sir," she said.

"Then neither do I condemn you," Jesus declared. "Go now and leave your life of sin."

The crowd gathered not by ones and twos, but as though they were drawn in as one object. As soon as Jesus was seen and His name was mentioned, the people moved en masse to listen to Him. As they drew near to Him, He sat down and began to teach. Many of them found renewal in His words. Some found, for the first time, that they wanted to honor God, not simply that they felt compelled to.

The Pharisees and the teachers of the law were always anxious to get to the explanation of what the people *must* do. All they seemed to care about was making sure those listening knew their responsibilities and the penalties for breaking God's laws and their traditions.

Jesus had been teaching for some time when a commotion across the courtyard caught His attention. As He looked at a small group coming toward Him, the whole crowd turned. They saw the collection of Pharisees and teachers of the law advancing. Clearly intent on reaching Jesus, they nearly willed the crowd to part so they could make their way through. The crowd obeyed the silent command and in moments the band stood in front of Jesus.

They brought a woman forward and stood her in front of Jesus. Four expressions could be identified on the faces of those present. The faces of the Pharisees and teachers of the law revealed their attitude toward Jesus and the woman they had caught. The crowd who had been listening to Jesus all wore expressions of nervous anticipation. Jesus's own face showed a mixture of compassion and outrage. And the woman's shame and fear could both be seen clearly in the tears that streamed down her cheeks.

The Pharisees spoke about her with vulgar candor as though she were nothing more than a specimen to be studied, an animal to be examined. "Teacher, this woman was caught in the act of adultery. In the Law Moses commanded us to stone such women. Now what do you say?"

Murmurs rolled through the crowd. The law was clear. If she was guilty, she deserved capital punishment by stoning. Jesus had a way of understanding the law that no one there had ever heard before. He never violated the law or set it aside, but His teaching seemed to go beyond and reinterpret it all at the same time. It was clear that this was a test, maybe even a trap.

Everyone waited. Jesus said nothing. He looked at each of the men in the group that had brought the woman and held their gaze for just a moment.

He stretched His hand toward the dirt, paused, then began to trace His finger across the ground. As He scrawled, the teachers of the law pressed Him for an answer. They quoted Moses, talked about the purity of Israel, and the need to punish sin.

He pulled His finger from the dirt and looked at His work. The Pharisees and teachers of the law fell silent and looked at what He had done.

Those in the front of the crowd could see; those behind strained to glimpse it. He stood and said, "Let any one of you who is without sin be the first to throw a stone at her," and He returned His finger to the dirt and began writing again.

The silence was the definition of *uncomfortable*. He hadn't defied the law. He hadn't said not to stone her. But His requirement for participation was extraordinary. No one thought of his neighbor; each was consumed by the thoughts of his own disqualifications. The woman watched in growing amazement as the crowd began to dissipate. Melting and shrinking. She saw the men who brought her drop their eyes and begin to walk away.

Jesus was left alone with the woman. The irony was thick. The only one who was qualified to throw the first stone had challenged and disbanded those who wanted to throw them. He straightened and looked at her. When she told Him that no one had condemned her, His reply told her that she was truly safe, "Then neither do I condemn you," Jesus declared. "Go now and leave your life of sin." She left, grateful for mercy and determined to honor His instructions.

REFLECT

It's easy to ignore our own sin when it's just us who's paying attention to it. And it's even easier to see the sin of someone else. How often do you ask God to help you see your sins? For what would you be dragged before Jesus in need of His forgiveness? How frequently do you ask God to give you His eyes of mercy with which to view others? Take some time to thank Jesus that, though He could condemn you, He has acted in great mercy toward you.

———————

Merciful Savior, forgive us for being short-sighted, eager to expose the sins of others. Forgive us for wanting what makes us comfortable and right. Help us to look at ourselves before we look at the sins of others.

Give me the courage to ruthlessly examine my heart, mind, and actions to see where I break Your heart. Help me to see my way forward to follow You and to help others do the same. Amen.

28

THE CONFIDENT

Luke 10:25–37

On one occasion an expert in the law stood up to test Jesus. "Teacher," he asked, "what must I do to inherit eternal life?"

"What is written in the Law?" he replied. "How do you read it?"

He answered, "'Love the Lord your God with all your heart and with all your soul and with all your strength and with all your mind'; and, 'Love your neighbor as yourself.'"

"You have answered correctly," Jesus replied. "Do this and you will live."

But he wanted to justify himself, so he asked Jesus, "And who is my neighbor?"

In reply Jesus said: "A man was going down from Jerusalem to Jericho, when he was attacked by robbers. They stripped him of his clothes, beat him and went away, leaving him half dead. A priest happened to be going down the same road, and when he saw the man, he passed by on the other side. So too, a Levite, when he came to the place and saw him, passed by on the other side. But a Samaritan, as he traveled, came where the man was; and when he saw him, he took pity on him. He went to him and bandaged his wounds, pouring on oil and wine. Then he put the man on his own donkey, brought him to an inn and took care of him. The next day he took out two denarii and gave them to the innkeeper. 'Look after him,' he said, 'and when I return, I will reimburse you for any extra expense you may have.'

"Which of these three do you think was a neighbor to the man who fell into the hands of robbers?"

The expert in the law replied, "The one who had mercy on him."

Jesus told him, "Go and do likewise."

God's blessing seemed to have been on him from his earliest days, and he had succeeded in everything to which he had put his mind. So, he had turned his mind toward God. What higher profession could an Israelite seek? There was nothing nobler than to study the law given through Moses and then to teach others its meaning. It was a long and difficult road of study, requiring diligence and discipline. But for him, no other path would satisfy; everything else felt too little, too low.

Like he had with every other aspiration in his young life, he succeeded, quicky surpassing his peers. His memory, nearly eidetic, consumed the texts. He could repeat them flawlessly and quote the commentaries and applications. But his sharp mind also saw new ideas in the text, new levels of meaning and application. These, however, he did not share—tradition was the unspoken and inviolable law.

His rise to the top was spectacular but nothing below his expectations. To be an expert in the law was the fulfillment of his potential. He was at the top looking down. And then *He* came.

Jesus was being talked about all over Israel. The miracles were indeed an impressive sign that He was from God, but there was something unsettling about His teaching. He broke tradition. He reinterpreted the laws. He challenged the words of the elders and claimed to be honoring the law while appearing to break it. Despite the miracles, something seemed off about Jesus, and he, the expert in the law, decided he would be the one to expose Jesus. A test was in order.

Days were spent thinking about Jesus and what He had said, the teachings He had given. What question, what issue, would reveal Jesus's shortcomings? He spent hours comparing the deep issues of the law with what he knew of Jesus. Finally, it came to him, an issue that was based in the law and yet transcended it. Now to find Jesus and ask Him.

When his opportunity came, he was seated in the crowd listening to Jesus teach. He had to admit, there was something about Jesus; His words stirred something deep within him.

He shook himself and focused on the task before him. He stood up from his place in the crowd. "Teacher," he asked, "what must I do to inherit eternal life?"

Jesus, however, was not without craftiness of

His own. The question, so carefully considered to put Jesus on the spot, was turned back on the asker. But the expert was not shaken. He gave the answer that he would have accepted from Jesus—loving God and loving neighbor. And it was Jesus who affirmed him.

In a moment the entire plan seemed to be burning itself up all around him. He was not supposed to be the one put on the spot. Attempting to salve his ego, he asked a second question. He wanted to see where Jesus would draw the line. "And who is my neighbor?"

But the story that Jesus told in response, frustrated, offended, and shamed the expert. He could not, in the end, bring himself to name the person he was supposed to emulate in showing kindness to his neighbor. Jesus had made a Samaritan the hero of the tale. A Samaritan was the one who set the standard, and the Jews in the story, both devotees of the law, were shown to be lacking. Jesus may as well have said, "You, sir, have never been a true neighbor." Jesus's larger point was that love for neighbor is not about checking off boxes, but helping anyone in need who comes across your path. However, it was dressed in language to show just how far the expert really was from eternal life.

Jesus's parting words seared the point home: "Go and do likewise." Go and be like this Samaritan.

REFLECT

It can be easy to think we have following Jesus figured out. Of course, there are areas in which we can grow, but we imagine we've got the basics and the general direction down pat. When was the last time you allowed Jesus to challenge the way you view issues, whether theological or social? More practically, how do you care for your neighbor? When you last saw someone in need, did you help them or did you merely shake your head in sympathy? Or worse, did you tell yourself they're simply suffering the consequences of their own choices? How will you respond the next time you see someone in need?

Merciful Lord, if our neighbor is anyone we encounter whose need we can meet, then we are guilty, nearly daily, of ignoring the needs of our neighbors. We rarely love our neighbor as we love ourselves.

Forgive me for the selfishness and arrogance—even laziness—that keep me from helping those I could. Grant me greater vision to see people in need around me. Thank You for showing me what it means to love others. Help me to give of myself the way You have given Yourself for me. Amen.

29

THE DISTRACTED

Luke 10:38–42

As Jesus and his disciples were on their way, he came to a village where a woman named Martha opened her home to him. She had a sister called Mary, who sat at the Lord's feet listening to what he said. But Martha was distracted by all the preparations that had to be made. She came to him and asked, "Lord, don't you care that my sister has left me to do the work by myself? Tell her to help me!"

"Martha, Martha," the Lord answered, "you are worried and upset about many things, but few things are needed—or indeed only one. Mary has chosen what is better, and it will not be taken away from her."

There was much to do. Guests demanded hospitality. It wasn't that the guests themselves were demanding. Rather, it was the culture that demanded a proper table. Martha would make sure that while Jesus and His disciples were in her house, they would be comfortable and well cared for. Martha would see little rest during their stay.

Jesus was here, in her home. She was nearly bursting with pride at the honor of it all, and her delight propelled her busily through her home, organizing and preparing. For every task she crossed off the list, she discovered there were two additional things to do. This had to be a memorable stay. Jesus was not just any teacher. Martha, Mary, and their brother believed He could indeed be the Messiah, the hope of Israel. To be a part, even a small part, of His work was an opportunity not to be taken lightly.

As Martha toiled, she realized she was working alone. The responsibilities of hosting thirteen additional guests fell to her, but she should not be working alone. Mary should be with her, helping to care for their needs—cleaning, preparing food, organizing quarters. But she was alone, shouldering all the work herself.

Mary was not hiding, and she was not shirking her responsibilities. She had simply joined with the group sitting around Jesus, listening to Him teach. Any thoughts of meal preparation or bedding were far from her mind as she heard Jesus speak of the kingdom. Mary was enthralled. Her singular focus was Jesus and His words. Nothing could pull her away from her place at His feet.

Martha, however, only heard pieces of Jesus's teaching. Words and phrases occasionally penetrated her task-focused mind. How she would have enjoyed sitting at the Lord's feet and hearing Him speak, but that was not her place, and it shouldn't have been Mary's. There was too much to be done, and she was the one who needed to do it, apparently alone. How could Mary leave her to do all the work?

There Mary sat, listening, unconcerned with anything else. It was finally too much. She had been working alone for too long, and Mary was simply sitting at the Master's feet. "Lord, don't you care that my sister has left me to do the work by myself? Tell her to help me!"

Her exhaustion and frustration were obvious. How could Jesus not care that Martha was working so hard and Mary was not helping her? Did He think the work was that easy or that light? Everything she was doing was for Him and His disciples, yet He did not tell Mary to help with the things that needed to be done to make His own stay comfortable. Martha thought Mary's place was with her, and she thought Jesus should think the same. But Jesus's reply froze her.

"Martha, Martha," the Lord answered, "you are worried and upset about many things, but few things are needed—or indeed only one. Mary has chosen what is better, and it will not be taken away from her."

"Worried and upset"? "Mary has chosen the better"? For the first time, Martha considered the work she was doing might not need to be done at all. Was that possible? Jesus seemed to be saying so—that all the preparations and work of hosting guests was indeed far less important than simply sitting with Jesus and hearing His words. Martha's mind warred at the idea. Who would take care of the preparations? Who would prepare the meal?

A thought occurred to her. What was the result of each of their paths, hers and her sister's? What would they have to show for how they spent their time? Martha would have the memory and pride of being a good hostess, of knowing she had cared for Jesus in a tangible way. Mary would have Jesus Himself. What Mary heard as she sat at Jesus's feet, what she learned from Him would be hers forever. Her life would be transformed.

Suddenly the meal seemed less important. The cleaning could wait. It could all wait. Jesus said there was only one thing that was important: Him. Martha had made the wrong choice, but she did not have to continue making it. Martha, too, could choose the better.

REFLECT

It's a familiar question but one that deserves to be asked. Do you let doing things for Jesus get in the way of being with Jesus? Perhaps your busyness isn't even for Jesus. Maybe it's just the busyness of life. What are your priorities? When do you question them? Perhaps you allow the categories to blur and think of activities as spending time with Jesus. Do the things that you do fall in the "needed" category? Which thing gets ignored first when life is too full—time with Jesus or the tasks that overwhelm your to-do list?

Jesus, life is busy, and we can be worried and upset about many things—things we consider important, things that seem necessary. But sometimes these things can distract us from what is truly important: spending time with You.

Forgive me for my disordered priorities, for being distracted by my lists of tasks to accomplish. Help me to think carefully about how I spend my time and the significance I place on the activities that fill my days. Give me discernment where needed to sort out the immediate and necessary from all the rest. Grant me the discipline to carry out what I have carefully thought through and decided is important. Help me to see that spending time with You impacts everything else I do. Help me to remember that what I gain in Your presence can never be taken away from us. Amen.

30

THE
FIXATED

John 11:17–27, 32–37

On his arrival, Jesus found that Lazarus had already been in the tomb for four days. Now Bethany was less than two miles from Jerusalem, and many Jews had come to Martha and Mary to comfort them in the loss of their brother. When Martha heard that Jesus was coming, she went out to meet him, but Mary stayed at home.

"Lord," Martha said to Jesus, "if you had been here, my brother would not have died. But I know that even now God will give you whatever you ask."

Jesus said to her, "Your brother will rise again."

Martha answered, "I know he will rise again in the resurrection at the last day."

Jesus said to her, "I am the resurrection and the life. The one who believes in me will live, even though they die; and whoever lives by believing in me will never die. Do you believe this?"

"Yes, Lord," she replied, "I believe that you are the Messiah, the Son of God, who is to come into the world."

When Mary reached the place where Jesus was and saw him, she fell at his feet and said, "Lord, if you had been here, my brother would not have died."

When Jesus saw her weeping, and the Jews who had come along with her also weeping, he was deeply moved in spirit and troubled. "Where have you laid him?" he asked.

"Come and see, Lord," they replied.

Jesus wept.

Then the Jews said, "See how he loved him!"

But some of them said, "Could not he who opened the eyes of the blind man have kept this man from dying?"

Lazarus had gotten sick, very sick. It was almost as if his sisters could sit and watch his decline in real time. But despair never set in.

They knew there was someone who could cure Lazarus: Jesus. Jesus could heal Lazarus, no matter what illness had overtaken his body. And He would. They all knew it. For all that had been brought to Him, they had never known Jesus not to heal someone. Not only was Jesus a miracle worker who had healed many others, He was also a friend, and He loved Lazarus.

Mary and Martha had sent word to Jesus as soon as they knew Lazarus would not recover on his own. "When Jesus arrives, He will heal Lazarus," they told each other. In his lucid moments, they reassured Lazarus that they had sent word to Jesus, that He must be on His way, arriving at any moment. The thought held them afloat until the end.

Lazarus died. Jesus did not heal him. He did not even come.

Death creates a fog around all grievers. Mary and Martha were suffocated by it. The funeral and burial preparations were accomplished with the help of friends from Jerusalem who had come to grieve with the sisters. Every conversation contained their refrain, *If only Jesus had come, Lazarus would not have died*. They did not understand, they could not imagine what had kept Jesus from the friend He loved.

The days after Lazarus was entombed and the stone rolled into place passed with both incredible speed and debilitating slowness. The grief was heavy, and the adjustment to their brother's absence caught the sisters in unexpected ways at nearly every moment.

The constant companion to Mary and Martha's grief was their confusion. Where was Jesus? If only He had been here, Lazarus would not have died. The pair kept repeating their question to each other and receiving the same broken stare in response. The mourners who came from Jerusalem to offer comfort watched this exchange with sympathy and concern. Their combined grief and confusion threatened to break them.

Four days after Lazarus was put in the tomb, a messenger entered the house and announced that Jesus was on His way. Mary and Martha, sitting together in the home, looked at each other. After a moment, Martha bolted for the door while Mary leaned back in her seat and stared at the now empty place across from her.

Martha's rush brought her face-to-face with

Jesus. She looked Him in the eyes and repeated the phrase that had tumbled around in her heart and taunted her from the moment she had sent word to Him that Lazarus was sick. "Lord," Martha said to Jesus, "if you had been here, my brother would not have died. But I know that even now God will give you whatever you ask."

Jesus offered no explanation for His delay. Instead, He told Martha that those who believe in Him will live, even though they die.

Returning to Mary, Martha quietly explained that Jesus was asking for her. Now she ran. She ran to the Lord. She ran to the man she hoped in and trusted. She ran from her grief and toward comfort.

Falling at Jesus's feet, she could not compose herself. Through her sobs, she too pieced together the phrase that her sister had uttered. Jesus looked at her with compassion. Those who had followed Mary thinking she was going to mourn at the tomb were weeping with her. Their grief and distress moved Jesus deeply.

He asked to be taken to where Lazarus had been laid to rest. When He saw the tomb, emotion overtook Him, and His love for Lazarus was put on display for all to see, as tears streaked His cheeks.

The display of raw emotion was both moving and confusing. Some of those gathered to mourn with the sisters wondered why Jesus, who had given sight to the blind, had not healed Lazarus and saved Himself—and Mary and Martha—such heartbreak.

REFLECT

The end of the story is the miraculous resurrection of Lazarus. But the refrain of the story is, If only Jesus had been here. The sisters and the crowd were fixated on the absence of Jesus and the power that could have healed Lazarus. What situations in your life have you asking Jesus why, or saying to Him, "If only you had done something"? Mary and Martha knew Jesus could save their brother, but they did not understand why He didn't. Do you know that Jesus can help you but question why He doesn't? Do you wonder, like the crowd, why some people seem to receive a blessing while others do not? How do you respond to Jesus's apparent absence?

Jesus, it is easy to admit that we do not know how, why, or when You choose to work. But it is sometimes difficult to accept that reality. We know You have the power to work in our lives and that Scripture encourages us to bring our requests to You. But the answer You give is not always the answer we seek.

I confess that it is easy to find myself saying, "If only You were here . . ." Help me to recognize that my ignorance is not the end of the story, that Your power and plans are not subject to my timing. Help me to trust You, even when I cannot understand. Amen.

31

THE ANTAGONISTIC

John 11:45–50; Mark 14:55–64

Therefore many of the Jews who had come to visit Mary, and had seen what Jesus did, believed in him. But some of them went to the Pharisees and told them what Jesus had done. Then the chief priests and the Pharisees called a meeting of the Sanhedrin.

"What are we accomplishing?" they asked. "Here is this man performing many signs. If we let him go on like this, everyone will believe in him, and then the Romans will come and take away both our temple and our nation."

Then one of them, named Caiaphas, who was high priest that year, spoke up, "You know nothing at all! You do not realize that it is better for you that one man die for the people than that the whole nation perish." . . .

The chief priests and the whole Sanhedrin were looking for evidence against Jesus so that they could put him to death, but they did not find any. Many testified falsely against him, but their statements did not agree.

Then some stood up and gave this false testimony against him: "We heard him say, 'I will destroy this temple made with human hands and in three days will build another, not made with hands.'" Yet even then their testimony did not agree.

Then the high priest stood up before them and asked Jesus, "Are you not going to answer? What is this testimony that these men are bringing against you?" But Jesus remained silent and gave no answer.

Again the high priest asked him, "Are you the Messiah, the Son of the Blessed One?"

"I am," said Jesus. "And you will see the Son of Man sitting at the right hand of the Mighty One and coming on the clouds of heaven."

The high priest tore his clothes. "Why do we need any more witnesses?" he asked.

"You have heard the blasphemy. What do you think?"

They all condemned him as worthy of death.

The band of men entered the hall with a distinct purpose. Those in front confidently leading the way, and those in the rear whispered excitedly about what was to come. The man in the middle was the cause and solution to all of it.

With His head bowed and His hands clasped in front of Him, He was unassuming at the most aggressive evaluation. What did they want with Him? They wanted Him dead. Why? He was, at least by appearances, anything but threatening.

But appearances can be deceiving. Jesus was a threat, especially in the eyes of this group. This was the Sanhedrin, the ruling council of the Jewish people, a group comprised of religious leaders, both Pharisees and Sadducees. To these men, Jesus was more than a nuisance; He was putting the nation in peril: "Here is this man performing many signs. If we let him go on like this, everyone will believe in him, and then the Romans will come and take away both our temple and our nation."

The thought of losing the temple—their identity,

their connection to God—pushed this group to the point of panic. When catastrophic change threatened, their response revealed a great deal about what the members of the Sanhedrin held most dear.

"You know nothing at all! You do not realize that it is better for you that one man die for the people than that the whole nation perish," said Caiaphas, high priest and leader of the Sanhedrin. It was self-protection: sacrifice one for the sake of the many.

Now, inside the palace of the high priest, this threat stood. His activity and, in their minds, His very life posed a risk to their way of life and their existence as a nation. As the religious authorities, it was their responsibility to look out for and protect the best interests of Israel. The course of action had already been decided. It was time to find the way to enact it.

Capital punishment was prescribed for a variety of sins in Israelite law. All they needed to do was to convict Him of one of those crimes. But the trial proved difficult, as Jesus had done nothing wrong.

In the end, it was one of the more serious crimes they laid at His feet: blasphemy. Blasphemy was as heinous and abhorrent as a crime could be. So appalling was blasphemy that immediate vigilante justice was sometimes attempted when it was identified.

Their question exposed their agenda, and there was little doubt as to their desired outcome.

"Are you the Messiah, the Son of the Blessed One?"

"I am."

Gavel bang. Guilty. Sentenced to death. "Why do we need any more witnesses? . . . You have heard the blasphemy. What do you think?" The agreement was unanimous. He was worthy of death.

If Jesus continued to do miracles, especially like raising people from the dead, "everyone" would believe in Him. Belief in Jesus was the risk. If Rome learned that the people of Israel had pledged their allegiance to a King other than Caesar, they would respond with force.

The Jewish ruling council faced a choice. They chose against Jesus in order to keep the temple. They chose against Him to protect the people. Their decision was intended to preserve their identity, security, and way of life.

REFLECT

The ability to choose is part of what makes us uniquely human. We face a multitude of choices every day, some relatively inconsequential and others with the power to change the course of our life. Some choices seem to have no wrong answer and others no right one. And our faith informs them all. But what happens when our faith doesn't seem to provide a clear answer? How do we decide when the choices we face are inscrutable? When was the last time you had to make a decision and were simply stumped for the right thing to do? Have you ever faced a choice that meant sacrificing for what was right?

———

Jesus, we're not often presented with choices that directly challenge our allegiance to You. Many of the choices we make don't seem to have any significant consequences for us or for our faith. But there are times when we depend on our faith to point us in the right direction. There are times when the culture or our country moves in a direction our conscience tells us is wrong. In those times, our ability to choose sits like a weight on our shoulders.

I want to make the right choices, but sometimes it's not easy to know what that right thing is. Sometimes, I struggle to know what to choose. Help me to see where You are in my decision making. Help me to weigh the consequences of my choices. I want my allegiance to You to be beyond doubt. Help me to choose wisely. Amen.

32

THE EXILED

Luke 17:11–19

Now on his way to Jerusalem, Jesus traveled along the border between Samaria and Galilee. As he was going into a village, ten men who had leprosy met him. They stood at a distance and called out in a loud voice, "Jesus, Master, have pity on us!"

When he saw them, he said, "Go, show yourselves to the priests." And as they went, they were cleansed.

One of them, when he saw he was healed, came back, praising God in a loud voice. He threw himself at Jesus' feet and thanked him—and he was a Samaritan.

Jesus asked, "Were not all ten cleansed? Where are the other nine? Has no one returned

to give praise to God except this foreigner?"
Then he said to him, "Rise and go; your faith
has made you well."

L ife in a leper colony was not what any of them
would have chosen. But it did have its perks.
For the members, the colony provided contact,
closeness, relationships after a fashion. It was a
place to belong for those plagued with a terrible
disease, the social implications of which rivaled
the actual physical symptoms for severity.

The men shared what they could with one another and offered each other the comfort of deep
empathy. There are few things that comfort more
than knowing someone understands exactly what
you are going through. In an odd way, this small
community of exiles offered a deeper sense of belonging than any community the men had previously been a part of. But even that silver lining was
thin and dull on a forebodingly dark storm cloud.

In their condition, these lepers were required
to isolate from the community until the afflic-
tion passed, if it ever did. Some in the group had
been there for a very long time. Others were new
additions, the wound caused by their situation

still open and raw. Any adjustment to life in the community was routinely hampered by the hopeful expectation of leaving soon. But, as of yet, no one had left the community. The malady was unwilling to let go and would remain with each of them for the rest of their lives, the duration of which would most likely be determined by the disease.

Though there was always the hope of returning to home and family, each one nursed a secret resignation to their fate.

Word of Jesus reached the small band of exiles. A miracle worker had arrived in Israel. No disease seemed beyond His ability to heal. They heard reports of blindness, deafness, and paralysis being healed, demons being exorcised. No one needed to ask whether or not it would be possible for Jesus to heal them. The new rush of hope was nearly instantaneous and overwhelming. The only thing they needed to discuss was how to find and approach Jesus.

The more they heard of Him, the higher their hopes rose. Surely Jesus *could* heal them. But would He? Stories of His miracles seemed so frequent that they supposed He must be healing nearly everyone who came to Him with any sort of infirmity.

They gathered along the road, careful to keep their distance from those who might come along, and then they waited. Patience and determination was rewarded when they saw a group of travelers coming down the road. When the miracle worker's presence was confirmed by some in the group, the lepers rushed toward Him, calling out to Him before He entered the village.

"Jesus, Master, have pity on us!" Their need was obvious; Jesus's action, immediate.

He called back to them, "Go, show yourselves to the priests."

Immediately they all turned and ran to do just what Jesus had said. Showing themselves to the priest, according to the law, was only done after the disease retreated completely. If Jesus was sending them to do that, they were already cleansed—or would be by the time they stood before the priest. It was a dead run, each man going as quickly as his legs would take him. Visions of reunions with family and friends pulled them forward.

One man, unable to keep from examining his

skin, slowed from a run to a walk and then stood still, marveling at the smooth blemish-free skin on his arms. Raising his hand to his face, he felt . . . nothing. The lesions and sores that had, just moments ago, determined his lifestyle were gone. He wobbled slightly as his knees buckled beneath him. It was too much, too wonderful. Turning, he ran back to Jesus, joy shining from his face and gratitude bursting from his heart. His voice carried through the countryside as he shouted the praises of God.

This time he did not keep his distance. There was no need. He threw himself at Jesus's feet, wrapped his arms around Jesus's legs, and wept in gratitude. His words were a jumbled, barely intelligible combination of thanks and praises to God.

Jesus looked down at him, compassion in His eyes and voice, "Were not all ten cleansed? Where are the other nine? Has no one returned to give praise to God except this foreigner?" He was correct—the man kneeling before Him was a Samaritan, a despised outsider to Israel. Yet he was the only one to return with gratitude for the miracle Jesus had given them. An outsider was the only one to recognize what had truly happened and to connect with Jesus on a deeper level.

"Rise and go; your faith has made you well." The Samaritan's gratitude was an expression of faith. That faith had given him a healing that transcended the cleansing of his skin and brought him into the kingdom of God.

REFLECT

There is an important link between faith and gratitude. The latter often serves as an expression of the former. Jesus's words to the grateful Samaritan reveal that relationship. What are the things for which you are most grateful to God? How do you express that gratitude? Are there things in your life that perhaps you take for granted—things for which you've never bothered to turn back and thank Jesus? What practice might you adopt to remind yourself of the many blessings God has given you?

Healing Savior, sometimes it can be easy to focus on the negative things that happen in life. When we do that, we can lose sight of the many good things You have provided. And even when we do remember those good gifts, we can quickly take them for granted, leaving gratitude by the wayside.

Forgive me for my ingratitude and for the times when I sin in arrogance, thinking my good things have been wrought by my own hands. Help me to remember Your goodness to me. I want my faith to express itself in gratefulness. Prompt my heart to respond in praise and thanksgiving when I recognize Your good gifts in my life. Amen.

33

THE ZEALOUS

Luke 22:47–51

While he was still speaking a crowd came up, and the man who was called Judas, one of the Twelve, was leading them. He approached Jesus to kiss him, but Jesus asked him, "Judas, are you betraying the Son of Man with a kiss?"

When Jesus' followers saw what was going to happen, they said, "Lord, should we strike with our swords?" And one of them struck the servant of the high priest, cutting off his right ear.

But Jesus answered, "No more of this!" And he touched the man's ear and healed him.

Their sleep was not deep, nor was it restful, and it wasn't wanted. But when a mind, exhausted by sorrow, orders the body to sleep, the body obeys. Peter, James, and John stood and stretched, sheepish that they could not offer Jesus the support He had asked for.

Peter could not look Jesus in the eye. Mere hours before, he had pledged his loyalty, even if it meant death, and now he couldn't even stay awake to pray with his Master. He was ashamed. He felt, and said, that he would stand strong, even if all the others did not. But the grass impressions on his cheek told a story of weakness and vulnerability.

Jesus, too, looked tired. But His was not a tiredness from too little sleep. It was a tiredness of mind and spirit. The weariness, however, was merely surface. Beneath it was a strength that showed Jesus was prepared for what was to come. What that was Peter did not know, but he determined to stand with Jesus.

The events and discussion of the night had unsettled all of the disciples. Nothing had been normal or encouraging.

Jesus had washed their feet. The Master had taken the role of a slave. Peter remembered that with a twinge of embarrassment. He had objected, only to be scolded, and when he tried to embrace the idea, he had gone too far and was gently corrected.

There was talk of Jesus's body and blood and a new covenant. Peter was not alone in his thoughts returning to Jesus's words over the bread and the cup.

Then there was the revelation of betrayal. How could any of them turn their back on Jesus? They had been together for so long. They had all looked around, each convinced in his own heart that it must be one of the others.

Confusion and sadness only deepened when Jesus began to talk about going away. This was too much. They had given up everything to follow Him, and now He was telling them His time was drawing to a close—that it was time for Him to go. Go where? What were they supposed to do without Him?

Then they had come here, to the garden. Jesus was obviously distressed. This pushed Peter and the others to the edge of themselves. They had never seen Jesus like this. What were they to do?

Pray. Jesus asked them to pray. But they could not. Closing their eyes proved too tempting, and they succumbed to fitful sleep, plagued by dreams of betrayal and of Jesus leaving.

Now they stood with Jesus, ashamed of their failure to stay awake. Peter resolving, again, to stay true to Jesus. That's when the crowd approached. Crowds were nothing new to Jesus and His disciples, but this one seemed different.

They stood in a close group with Jesus out in front. The eleven disciples tried to understand what was happening. Their confusion found temporary relief when they glimpsed Judas, one of their own, at the front of the crowd. But that comfort was short-lived. Sudden realization dawned when they heard Jesus greet Judas.

"Judas, are you betraying the Son of Man with a kiss?" Betrayal! It was Judas! It was all happening just as Jesus said. Now the torches looked menacing rather than illuminating. In their light the disciples saw clubs and swords. This was not a crowd coming to listen to Jesus teach, nor was this a crowd of people in need of healing.

Peter saw what was happening. The betrayer had led them here, and they were going to take Jesus! Everything crashed on him in a moment: anger at Judas, his promises of loyalty, his failure to support his friend and Master. It was too much. This was the moment he would keep his promise. This was the moment he would prove himself to Jesus, to the others, and to himself.

"Shall we strike?" But there was no waiting for a reply. Peter's blade sliced through the air. Fishermen are not soldiers, and Peter's wild swing took off the ear of the high priest's servant.

Jesus's voice stopped Peter's follow-up swing in mid-stroke. It froze everyone. "No more of this!" They all watched as Jesus did what Jesus had done for years: heal. He reached out and restored the man's ear. Uncertainty confused Peter's thoughts. Jesus healed someone who had come to arrest Him! Jesus didn't permit Peter to defend Him. What was he to do now?

The others had fled. The crowd was leaving with Jesus. Peter thought he had failed; they had taken Jesus.

REFLECT

Peter was zealous in his commitment to follow Jesus and his commitment to protect Jesus. He was prepared to fight. Sometimes it feels like the world, society, and culture are all trying to take Jesus away. How do you respond? Do you draw your sword and go on the attack, attempting to kill or maim (figuratively, of course) those who are trying to take your Jesus away? What if Jesus wants us to stop our attempts to "keep Him"? What if we have made wounds that He wants to heal? Peter thought he was doing the right thing. He was following through on his promise to stand with Jesus, but it was not what Jesus wanted. It was not the way Jesus worked. What if we are similarly misguided in some of our attempts to defend Jesus? How would we know?

God of Surprises, You work in ways that are surprising and difficult to understand, but they reveal Your character and Your plans as uniquely Yours. Sometimes, perhaps often, we get both the plan and the execution wrong. It can feel like the world is trying to take our Jesus away. We confess that sometimes we draw our swords and attack. We slash and cut.

Forgive me for the times when my sword has gone against You and Your work. Forgive me for the harm I have caused in my zeal to protect what I think I need to protect. Please reach out and heal the wounds I have inflicted in my eagerness. Help me remember that those who come against You are people who need to know You—and that my sword is perhaps not the best introduction. Help me to be like You when faced with an "enemy." Grant me the peace to know Your plan is unfolding when I may not be able to see it. Amen.

THE
FAITHLESS

Luke 22:54–62

Then seizing him, they led him away and took him into the house of the high priest. Peter followed at a distance. And when some there had kindled a fire in the middle of the courtyard and had sat down together, Peter sat down with them. A servant girl saw him seated there in the firelight. She looked closely at him and said, "This man was with him."

But he denied it. "Woman, I don't know him," he said.

A little later someone else saw him and said, "You also are one of them."

"Man, I am not!" Peter replied.

About an hour later another asserted, "Certainly this fellow was with him, for he is a Galilean."

Peter replied, "Man, I don't know what you're talking about!" Just as he was speaking, the rooster crowed. The Lord turned and looked straight at Peter. Then Peter remembered the word the Lord had spoken to him: "Before the rooster crows today, you will disown me three times." And he went outside and wept bitterly.

He stared at the blood on his hand. There were a few spots on his garment as well. It was more than he would have thought. Peter had no idea there was so much blood in an ear. He absent-mindedly wiped his hand on his thigh as he watched the mob head toward the high priest's house, Jesus at the center.

He was frozen for a moment, unsure of what to do. Jesus had stopped him from fighting any further. The temple soldiers tried to grab more of them, but everyone scattered, running terrified into the night. Peter just stood there in disbelief. All of this in the space of a few moments.

Now he was alone.

Before he knew it, almost without his command, his legs were moving. He was following the group who had taken Jesus. The movement brought focus, purpose, but not necessarily clarity. He followed at a distance. His courage could be mustered only so far. He crept along, keeping out of sight of the mob. But his caution may have been unwarranted; the crowd had their prize; they were unconcerned with what was behind them.

A torrent of thoughts crashed through his mind. Nothing helped. He couldn't sort anything out. Jesus had slipped away from murderous intentions before. Why not this time? All of the previous confrontations with the religious elites ended with Jesus having the upper hand; this one felt different. It was different. There was no testing, no probing question designed to trick Him. The time for conversation was over. There was simply aggression and physical confrontation.

A series of statements crashed through Peter's mind: "The Son of Man must suffer many things and be rejected by the elders, the chief priests and the teachers of the law, and that he must be killed and after three days rise again" (Mark 8:31). "The Son of Man is going to be delivered into the hands of men. They will kill him, and after three days he will rise" (Mark 9:31). "The

Son of Man will be delivered over to the chief priests and the teachers of the law. They will condemn him to death and will hand him over to the Gentiles to be mocked and flogged and crucified. On the third day he will be raised to life!" (Matthew 20:18–19).

Elders, chief priests, hands of men, killed. Peter fixated on the words; the last phrases about rising meaningless in the terror of the moment. Were Jesus's words coming true? Was this really happening?

He followed the crowd to the courtyard of the high priest's home. He looked himself over, obvious blood would start a conversation he'd rather not have. His hands were clean enough and his dark garments had absorbed the blood he had wiped on them. Still, he waited. Soon, a fire was kindled that cast dancing shadows around the courtyard. The warmth of the fire and his curiosity over Jesus's fate drew him in.

Taking a seat close to the fire, he stretched his hands toward it, wiggling his fingers toward its warmth. He kept in the shadows as much as he could, listening for any word, trying to figure out what was happening to Jesus. His eyes locked for a moment with a servant girl's. He quickly looked away, but she continued to stare.

She pointed at him. "This man was with him," she said to everyone and no one. Peter's heart froze. He was cornered. What would they do to him? He had to stay here, to stay close to Jesus. He could not be taken; he could not leave. He had to stay safe. Denial seemed the best choice.

The conversation continued, and Peter tried to settle his nerves. It didn't work. Tension filled the air as Jesus and the religious leaders continued their . . . whatever was happening; Peter couldn't quite understand it.

Another person noticed Peter sitting there. Despite his efforts, he was not escaping scrutiny. "You also are one of them." Everyone was looking at them. They had heard the girl's earlier question. He was afraid, and his fear gave volume and force to his words, "Man, I am not!" The startled questioner backed away, but his expression revealed he was not convinced.

Minutes passed, first fifteen, then thirty. Peter began to calm. More time passed. But the peace lasted only an hour. A man confronted him.

He had pegged him as a Galilean. That gave him away.

Peter needed to escape the suspicion. He adamantly denied knowing Jesus.

Three things happened in the moment he finished speaking: a rooster crowed, Jesus's eyes met his, and Jesus's prediction returned to Peter's mind. It was too much. Peter broke. He proved faithless. He had disowned and denied Jesus.

He left the fire, the courtyard, the crowd, and Jesus behind. He wept bitterly into the night as he ran.

REFLECT

Conviction is a difficult thing. Being broken by our own sin, whether deliberate sin or not, is never easy. It is a stark reminder of our failures and weakness. How does the Spirit convict you of your sin? What do you experience and when do you experience it? Is it immediate? Delayed? Sometimes both? How do you respond when you are convicted? Have you been given the opportunity to side with Jesus? What did you do?

Jesus, though to us our sins don't usually feel as serious as Peter's denial, they do break Your heart, just as Peter's words did, and they place a barrier between us. There are even some times when we confess but do not repent—admit our wrong doing, but fail to make any changes.

Forgive me for harboring my sin, for keeping the things in my life that appeal to me but You have commanded against. Thank You for the conviction Your Spirit brings and the path to restoration that it opens. Help me to listen when the Spirit whispers conviction to my heart. Enable me to behave like a child of God. Amen.

35

THE
CURIOUS

John 18:33–38

Pilate then went back inside the palace, summoned Jesus and asked him, "Are you the king of the Jews?"

"Is that your own idea," Jesus asked, "or did others talk to you about me?"

"Am I a Jew?" Pilate replied. "Your own people and chief priests handed you over to me. What is it you have done?"

Jesus said, "My kingdom is not of this world. If it were, my servants would fight to prevent my arrest by the Jewish leaders. But now my kingdom is from another place."

"You are a king, then!" said Pilate.

Jesus answered, "You say that I am a king. In fact, the reason I was born and came into the world is to testify to the truth. Everyone on the side of truth listens to me."

"What is truth?" retorted Pilate. With this he went out again to the Jews gathered there and said, "I find no basis for a charge against him."

Jesus and Pilate stood regarding one another. Pilate was the one with official authority. He was the one who could make things happen. He held life and death in his hands. In fact, that was the reason the Jewish council had brought Jesus here in the first place. They wanted Him executed.

Pilate met Jesus as a judge meets a defendant. This was a trial. Judge and accused stood face to face. This hearing revolved around one significant question. Pilate took the direct approach: "Are you the king of the Jews?" The answer would determine the outcome of this trial: verdict and sentencing.

After a bit of cat and mouse, an answer comes. "My kingdom is not of this world." In other words, "Yes, I am a king. But my kingdom isn't one you'll find on a map." Fastest court case in history. Open and shut. Guilty as charged.

Claim of kingship was sedition against Rome, punishable by death.

But Pilate wanted to release Jesus. "I find no basis for a charge against him." That stands in direct contradiction to the stated facts of the exchange. Pilate confronted Jesus with the charges, and in essence, Jesus pleaded guilty. Not only was there basis for the charge, there was evidence for conviction. But instead of the expected outcome, Pilate attempted to do the opposite.

What would lead a Roman official to suggest releasing someone who claimed to be a king?

"You are a king, then!" Pilate accepts His guilty plea.

"You say that I am a king. In fact, the reason I was born and came into the world is to testify to the truth. Everyone on the side of truth listens to me."

"What is truth?"

Jesus had a unique and intimate relationship with the truth. Pilate probably hadn't heard what Jesus had said about truth, and he may not have understood all the implications of his questions to Jesus.

After asking this fundamental question (with

no recorded response), Pilate returns to the Jewish leaders who brought Jesus to him and pronounces not just a not-guilty verdict, but claims that there isn't even a basis for a charge. This exchange is the hinge between the guilty plea and the suggestion of release. It is the reason for Pilate's verdict.

Jesus told Pilate that His kingdom was not of this world and that if it were, His subjects would fight for Him. It's possible that Pilate didn't see Jesus—King though He claimed to be—as a threat to Rome. (A kingdom not of this world cannot threaten the power of Rome.) Perhaps Pilate heard this answer and took pity on someone who seemed to be mentally unbalanced. A kingdom not of this world sounds like a kingdom in the imagination.

That scenario is plausible, and if true, it renders Pilate's question about truth to the first category—dismissive and sarcastic.

But this doesn't really explain the attempt to release Jesus. Even a mentally unstable man can pose a threat, especially if He has a following. The idea that Pilate would want to release someone who could gather a crowd and motivate them to action simply because Pilate thought he was delusional doesn't really stand up. Threats to Rome were serious business.

But what if the question was asked sincerely?

Jesus said there is an inseparable connection between the subjects of His kingdom and the truth. What if Pilate was not posing a philosophical question, but instead asking what characterized those who belonged to Jesus's kingdom. Jesus viewed both God's Word and Himself as fundamental expressions of the truth. Pilate was asking about Jesus's identity—Who are you, Jesus?

Pilate may not have been curious about the nature of truth, but instead about its relationship to those who follow Jesus. It's possible that Pilate was trying to reconcile a not-of-this-world kingdom with the claim that its subjects are indeed part of this world; Pilate was wondering how those subjects could be identified.

What Jesus said to Pilate is still true. Those on the side of truth listen to Him. What Pilate asked remains a significant and important question, not because truth is relative or debatable, but because truth identifies those who are in Jesus's kingdom. Those who want to know Him continue to ask questions. They continue to seek the truth.

REFLECT

Do you remember when you first met Jesus? Do you remember what it was like reading the stories in the Gospels and being surprised by what Jesus said and did? Do you still have a sense of curiosity about who Jesus is and what He does, or has familiarity bred contempt, or at least ambivalence? Sometimes the stories about Jesus become so well-known and loved that we begin to read over them to get to the point. How do you prepare yourself to read Scripture so that the stories are engaging and fresh? What would it be like to experience Scripture rather than study it? How do you continue to ask questions of the stories you know so well? How do you continue to seek the truth?

Jesus, we are so blessed to have the collected stories of Your time on earth. Knowing some of what You said and did during Your earthly life fills us with a sense of wonder. You are always worthy of our curiosity and our searching efforts. But it's easy to get to a point where we know the stories and our pursuit becomes routine rather than passion, obligation rather than exploration.

Have I lost some of the wonder I once had thinking about how You put on flesh and walked with humanity? That reality is behind the stories that I read in the Gospels, but it doesn't always feel intriguing. I may have become numb to Your [think of one thing about Jesus that you may have begun to take for granted because you "know Him"]. I wish I could have walked with You when Your feet stepped onto the water. Help me not to treat the stories about You as merely a vehicle to bring me to a theological point. Help me experience the same awe and wonder as those who said, "We have never seen anything like this!" (Mark 2:12). Amen.

36

THE CONVERT

Luke 23:32–43

Two other men, both criminals, were also led out with him to be executed. When they came to the place called the Skull, they crucified him there, along with the criminals—one on his right, the other on his left. Jesus said, "Father, forgive them, for they do not know what they are doing." And they divided up his clothes by casting lots.

The people stood watching, and the rulers even sneered at him. They said, "He saved others; let him save himself if he is God's Messiah, the Chosen One."

The soldiers also came up and mocked him. They offered him wine vinegar and said, "If you are the king of the Jews, save yourself."

There was a written notice above him, which read: THIS IS THE KING OF THE JEWS.

One of the criminals who hung there hurled insults at him: "Aren't you the Messiah? Save yourself and us!"

But the other criminal rebuked him. "Don't you fear God," he said, "since you are under the same sentence? We are punished justly, for we are getting what our deeds deserve. But this man has done nothing wrong."

Then he said, "Jesus, remember me when you come into your kingdom."

Jesus answered him, "Truly I tell you, today you will be with me in paradise."

The trio walked the road slowly, their somber demeanor in graphic contrast to the jeering mob that lined the streets. Three convicted men, all sentenced to death, walking to their place of execution, the Skull. The rock formation deserved its name; its visual appearance made its use inevitable. Countless criminals' sentences were carried out there. Crucifixion. The Romans were efficient, but in their efficiency, they retained their brutality.

Jesus was lifted up between the other two, naked and wracked with excruciating pain. The spikes driven through His hands and feet adding specific points of pain to a body already assaulted and suffering. He was pinned to the beams, held in place where everyone could see Him. The humiliation was part of the execution.

They hung there, the three of them. Their height from the crowd gave them an awkward secrecy. What they said, unless they raised their voices to be heard above the crowd, was shared only between them.

Jesus raised His head and uttered a phrase that shocked the two criminals and anyone else who may have been quiet enough and close enough to hear. "Father, forgive them, for they do not know what they are doing." There was more than a small amount of irony in the statement. The Jews and the Romans thought they knew what they were doing. No one knew better than the Romans what they were doing with a crucifixion. The Jewish leaders, too, knew what they were doing. They were purging their nation of a troublemaker.

But, of course, Jesus intended something far

deeper than what could be seen on the surface. The statement hung there with them. What it said about the speaker was as significant as its content.

Beneath them, the soldiers gambled for Jesus's clothes. Other than the seamless tunic, the clothes were not exceptionally nice, but casting lots for Jesus's wardrobe gave the soldiers something to do to entertain themselves, crucifixion having lost its intrigue long ago. Their cheers at their own game was an unsettlingly festive element in a gruesome scene.

Some in the watching crowd were hostile. They ridiculed Him, remembering the power He had used for others but now seemed to lack for Himself. "He saved others; let him save himself if he is God's Messiah, the Chosen One." "Save yourself!" they shouted in mockery.

The soldiers, too, took up the refrain. Offering Him wine vinegar, they jeered Him to save Himself if He was really the king of the Jews. A sign claiming the title had been nailed above His head. The words spoken in Pilate's hall were now hurled at Him with contempt.

"Save yourself!" The refrain came from everywhere.

The cry even came from those suffering beside Him. The criminal on His right called out for Jesus to save Himself and them. But the request was dipped in derision. Jesus looked just as helpless as he knew himself to be. *Save Yourself!*

They did not understand, not one of them, that He was, even now, saving others.

From His left came a surprising defense. This criminal had heard the stories of Jesus's exploits and His power. He, too, had joined in the derision earlier, suspecting that the one with the power to bring back the dead surely had the power to thwart execution. But the compassion of Jesus's request for forgiveness had snapped something inside of him. Jesus was suffering voluntarily and innocently. There was no defiance in Him. There was no enmity for the crowd who taunted Him.

Watching Jesus suffer an unjust fate and hearing the merciful words He uttered a moment before brought this criminal to a place of unexpected faith. He chastised the man who hung opposite him. Turning to Jesus, he made a different request. "Jesus, remember me when you come into your kingdom."

Jesus looked at him with pity and compassion.

Such faith. He responded, voice suffocated and hoarse with pain, "Truly I tell you, today you will be with me in paradise."

REFLECT

Jesus welcomed the faith of a dying criminal. It was a faith that motivated the man's final words and deeds. His conversion was a symbol that Jesus's saving work was being accomplished, that His restraint was bringing people into His kingdom. How does your faith find expression in the events of your life? How do you express to Jesus that you trust His power and His lordship, that you want to be remembered in His kingdom? Or, like Jesus's example, what does your sacrifice for the good of others look like? Where are you giving up your rights so that others may reap the benefits?

Jesus, thank You for welcoming our faith, no matter how small, weak, and uninformed. Thank You for remembering us though we are guilty as charged, deserving death.

Forgive me for the times I selfishly ask You to save me from something lesser, something inconsequential. Forgive me when I fail to appreciate the work You have done to bring me into Your kingdom. You have called me to model You in the world. Help me to see where my own agenda and desires keep me from giving what I can for the sake of others. Help me to place the good of others ahead of my own well-being. Amen.

37

THE SURPRISED

Luke 24:13–35

Now that same day two of them were going to a village called Emmaus, about seven miles from Jerusalem. They were talking with each other about everything that had happened. As they talked and discussed these things with each other, Jesus himself came up and walked along with them; but they were kept from recognizing him.

He asked them, "What are you discussing together as you walk along?"

They stood still, their faces downcast. One of them, named Cleopas, asked him, "Are you the only one visiting Jerusalem who does not know the things that have happened there in these days?"

"What things?" he asked.

"About Jesus of Nazareth," they replied. "He was a prophet, powerful in word and deed before God and all the people. The chief priests and our rulers handed him over to be sentenced to death, and they crucified him; but we had hoped that he was the one who was going to redeem Israel. And what is more, it is the third day since all this took place. In addition, some of our women amazed us. They went to the tomb early this morning but didn't find his body. They came and told us that they had seen a vision of angels, who said he was alive. Then some of our companions went to the tomb and found it just as the women had said, but they did not see Jesus."

He said to them, "How foolish you are, and how slow to believe all that the prophets have spoken! Did not the Messiah have to suffer these things and then enter his glory?" And beginning with Moses and all the Prophets, he explained to them what was said in all the Scriptures concerning himself.

As they approached the village to which they were going, Jesus continued on as if he were going farther. But they urged him strongly, "Stay with us, for it is nearly evening; the day is almost over." So he went in to stay with them.

When he was at the table with them, he took bread, gave thanks, broke it and began to give it to them. Then their eyes were opened and they recognized him, and he disappeared from their sight. They asked each other, "Were not our hearts burning within us while he talked with us on the road and opened the Scriptures to us?"

They got up and returned at once to Jerusalem. There they found the Eleven and those with them, assembled together and saying, "It is true! The Lord has risen and has appeared to Simon." Then the two told what had happened on the way, and how Jesus was recognized by them when he broke the bread.

The heaviness in their hearts seemed to weight even their feet. Steps were slow, plodding, difficult. The past few days had been long, lived in a haze of confusion that bordered on disbelief. And now, the events of the morning left the two already emotionally drained travelers on the verge of a complete breakdown.

What was happening? The Marys, Joanna, and a few others had said that Jesus was gone. They had seen the empty tomb, but they were not sad that Jesus was not there. Angels told them Jesus was alive! Peter and John had run to the tomb, only to find it empty. That they could confirm. But no angelic messenger had given them the same news that was given to the women.

The two men pondered these events as they walked. They spoke of their hopes that Jesus had been the one to restore Israel. They remembered all the things He had said about the kingdom of heaven, the miracles He had performed only deepened their hope that He was the Anointed One. They relived the terrible events of Jesus's arrest and crucifixion, the desperate and yawing hope that He would stop it somehow. But He hadn't.

Now He was simply gone. Angels had claimed He was alive, but no one had seen Him.

The stranger joined them and listened quietly while they talked to one another. The two noticed they were no longer traveling alone but hardly cared. Their minds were occupied with more important things. Until the stranger interrupted.

This man truly was a stranger. If He did not know what had happened in the last days, He must be the only one. Cleopas said as much. Still the stranger pressed. So the two travelers recounted the events that had been playing on a loop in their minds. They told Him about Jesus the prophet, the one whom they believed to be the restorer of Israel. They took turns recounting the night of the arrest and the trial. They described the hours that He hung on the cross until He died. Finally, they told Him of the body missing from the tomb and the heavenly message given to the women about Jesus being alive.

They were exhausted. The stranger could see it on their faces and hear it in the tremor of their voices.

He regarded them with sympathy, but His words were firm. They were foolish. They should have known that Messiah had to suffer these things. How could they not have understood what the prophets had written?

Cleopas and his companion were dumbstruck. Of all the things the stranger said, one stood out. He said that Messiah had to suffer. He was saying that Jesus was the Messiah. They were not wrong to put their hope in Him. But the stranger was not finished.

As they walked together, the stranger spoke to them of all that was written about Messiah from Moses and the Prophets. A familiar warmth flooded their hearts as they listened to the man explain Scripture to them in a way that was both new and ancient. It was something they had become accustomed to but, in the excitement of the moment, failed to recognize.

Their sorrow melted, and their footsteps lightened as they listened and became more and more convinced that Jesus was the Messiah. They marveled at all that was contained in Moses and the Prophets about Messiah and how Jesus fulfilled it all.

As they reached their destination, they urged the stranger to stay with them. His presence and teaching had been such a comfort to them; they wanted more.

Sitting down to their meal, the stranger blessed it and gave them the bread. In that moment, so simple and familiar, they were allowed to see.

Jesus was there with them. It was Him. The one they were now convinced was Messiah had been walking and talking with them! And then He was gone. But they knew. First by His words and how they moved in their hearts, and then by their sight. They knew it was Jesus, alive and well.

They hurried back to tell the others what they had heard and seen.

REFLECT

Cleopas and his companion were kept from recognizing Jesus as He walked with them, but also in their own reading of Scripture. Are there times in your life when it is possible you might not be recognizing Jesus? How might you be slow in understanding who Jesus is and what He is doing? Jesus explained to them that everything that happened to Him was there for them to see in Scripture, but they had missed it. How do you prepare to read Scripture so that you do not miss out?

Jesus, sometimes the events of life can overwhelm us to the point that it is hard to think about anything other than what is right in front of us. Thank You that in those moments when life is too much, You walk with us.

I confess that sometimes I am slow to see who You are. I am blinded by what I think are lost hopes and dreams. My own agenda and desires can, at times, keep me from understanding what is right in front of me. Help me to see You, to know You, and to understand Your work in this world. Amen.

38

THE DISILLUSIONED

John 21:2–7

Simon Peter, Thomas (also known as Didymus), Nathanael from Cana in Galilee, the sons of Zebedee, and two other disciples were together. "I'm going out to fish," Simon Peter told them, and they said, "We'll go with you." So they went out and got into the boat, but that night they caught nothing.

Early in the morning, Jesus stood on the shore, but the disciples did not realize that it was Jesus.

He called out to them, "Friends, haven't you any fish?"

"No," they answered.

He said, "Throw your net on the right side of the boat and you will find some." When they did, they were unable to haul the net in because of the large number of fish.

Then the disciple whom Jesus loved said to Peter, "It is the Lord!" As soon as Simon Peter heard him say, "It is the Lord," he wrapped his outer garment around him (for he had taken it off) and jumped into the water.

None of them knew what to do. In a matter of days, everything had been upended, changed. Nothing was the same. Their life of the last few years, gone. They were confused, scared, unsure, and insecure. What were they supposed to do now?

Everything they thought was coming, everything they thought was happening to them personally and for Israel had been derailed. Messiah had died and then risen from the dead. And even though Jesus was back, things were different. Jesus was different. Life didn't pick up from where it left off before He was crucified.

Three years they had spent together. The number of days they hadn't spent together was easy to count. They had shared everything. From the time Jesus called each of them, their lives had revolved around Him. He had taken them from what they were and made them into His disciples, teaching them about the kingdom of God, shaping their minds and hearts with His words. His miracles proved He was who He said He was—who they all thought He was, the Messiah of Israel.

There were more stories than they could remember. In the past few days, they found themselves reminiscing about something He said in His teaching or some miracle He had performed. Someone would remember some words or action, and they would all try to place it on a timeline. It was nearly impossible. They could remember the event well enough, but there were so many that the timeline in their minds lost its shape.

How many lepers had Jesus healed? The paralyzed man—was he by the pool or lowered through the roof? Both. The man through the roof also had his sins forgiven. So had the woman who invaded Simon's home and cried all over Jesus's feet. How many times had He fed a crowd? Walked on water? How many demons had been exorcized?

Life with Jesus had been exciting, unpredictable, but secure. He always made them feel secure. How could they not as long as He was with them? But then He was gone, was taken from them, and everything changed.

Seven of them were together, sitting at the table. They didn't know where the others were. In truth, they cared but didn't know what difference it would make if they were all together. The group had spent more and more time apart since that night in Gethsemane when they all fled. It was hard to see one another, to be around each other, to be reminded of how they had all failed Him.

Peter spoke up. "I'm going out to fish." It was the one thing he knew. It seemed the best path. He needed the comfort of the familiar now, even if it was the old familiar. It was a good idea. The others agreed to go along. They knew fishing.

But the fishing didn't provide the distraction they needed. It was a fishless night. Not a single fish found their nets. Now the sun was coming up, and the fishing was done. The men gathered their nets and prepared to return to shore.

As they turned their boat to head in, a figure on the beach called out to them. "Friends, haven't you any fish?" He followed their negative reply with instructions to lower their nets from the right side of the boat. They would find fish there.

It was worth a try. They lowered the net. Immediately the water frothed with the fish caught in the net. It was more than they could haul in. Peter had a flashback. This was familiar. He remembered another immense catch of fish after a fruitless night. That day was the day he was given a new career, fishing for men. The voice behind him brought Peter back to the present, "It is the Lord!"

With that, Peter was in the water, swimming to Jesus, leaving the others behind to wrestle with the fish.

The rest joined Peter and Jesus on the shore. They, too, knew it was Him. This was the third time they had seen Him. For a moment, for breakfast, life seemed normal again.

REFLECT

Have you ever found it confusing and difficult to follow Jesus? Have you ever had things not go the way you expected them to go? Perhaps you thought it was better to go back to something that was familiar and easier? How has Jesus reminded you that He has called you to something bigger, something better—a life lived in, through, and for Him?

———————

Jesus, sometimes we don't recognize You. In the busyness of life, we can fail to see who You are and what You are doing, and what You want us to do. Forgive us for being caught up in our own lives so deeply that we miss You.

Thank You that when I am confused, when I am unsure and do not know what to do, You come to me and remind me of Your calling on my life. Help me, like Peter, to come to You as soon as I recognize You, to leave behind what was keeping me from You. Amen.

39

THE REMORSEFUL

John 21:15–19

When they had finished eating, Jesus said to Simon Peter, "Simon son of John, do you love me more than these?"

"Yes, Lord," he said, "you know that I love you."

Jesus said, "Feed my lambs."

Again Jesus said, "Simon son of John, do you love me?"

He answered, "Yes, Lord, you know that I love you."

Jesus said, "Take care of my sheep."

The third time he said to him, "Simon son of John, do you love me?"

Peter was hurt because Jesus asked him the

third time, "Do you love me?" He said, "Lord, you know all things; you know that I love you."

Jesus said, "Feed my sheep. Very truly I tell you, when you were younger you dressed yourself and went where you wanted; but when you are old you will stretch out your hands, and someone else will dress you and lead you where you do not want to go." Jesus said this to indicate the kind of death by which Peter would glorify God. Then he said to him, "Follow me!"

When was it coming? The anticipation was excruciating. For brief moments, Peter allowed himself to think that maybe it wasn't coming. Then he would realize that if it did not come, he would have to force the issue. He could not go on like this. This was not a "pretend something didn't happen" issue. Something had happened. The fact that it had not been addressed yet did not mean that it was not important.

Peter glanced frequently at Jesus. His demeanor, expressions, conversation all seemed normal. But Peter could not help but think—know—something had to be there. If it was not for Jesus; it was for Peter.

His dreams and his waking thoughts had been plagued by the night in the garden and its aftermath. He had revisited the events time and time again, making different choices. The ultimate result was always the same, but his many relived paths took different routes there. Even in his fantasies, he could not stop the men from taking Jesus. He could not free Him from the guards; he could not stop the verdict or the execution.

The only thing Peter's fantasies truly accomplished was to deepen his regret. Walking through the different choices he could have made squeezed his heart in a vice of remorse.

His failure in the garden of Gethsemane was not a failure to protect Jesus; it was a failure to reflect Jesus. It was a failure possible only through a lack of understanding. He could learn; he could grow. But, as painful as a failure of understanding was after three years of walking with Jesus, it was not nearly as wounding as his failure in the courtyard.

Two memories tangled themselves in Peter's mind, taunting him with their intertwined images: There was the upper room, the Passover meal during which Jesus predicted Peter's denial and Peter insisted he would die first. And then there was the courtyard. Peter could hear himself deny knowing Jesus, and each time his own martyr bravado from the upper room would reverberate through his mind. "I don't know him!" *"Even if I have to die with you, I will never disown you."* Over and over on an endless loop. Peter's edges were beginning to fray.

He was startled back to reality when Jesus said his name. "Simon, son of John, do you love me more than these?" Jesus had called him Simon. That was unusual. Jesus had renamed him the very first time they met and he had either been Simon Peter or just Peter since then. Now he was Simon again. Peter understood what was happening. This was it. It was time. Tears pooled but did not fall.

Jesus was asking how much Peter loved Him, if he truly did love Him enough to sacrifice for Him. Peter answered honestly. Of course he loved Jesus.

"Feed my lambs."

But Jesus repeated the question. The exact same question. And Peter gave the exact same answer.

"Simon, do you love me?"

"Yes, Lord, I do love you."

"Take care of my sheep."

The question came a third time, and Peter understood the meaning behind the repetition, but it hurt all the same.

"Feed my sheep."

It was indirect, but they both knew what was happening. Jesus was healing Peter. This was a different kind of miracle, one that Peter had to participate in. Jesus's questions and His charge for Peter to care for His lambs told Peter that Jesus was still on his side. It was enough for Peter to balance the terrible sounds and images of his recent past. He could move forward now. He could breathe again.

Jesus continued to talk with Peter. The deep bond of trust was being repaired. It did not seem broken from Jesus's side. He had predicted the entire scenario. The effect on Peter, however, was disastrous. The weeping that occurred that fateful evening had recurred most evenings since. Peter and Jesus walked and talked, and Jesus again told him of his future, where and how he would go.

Jesus ended this conversation in much the same way their first conversation had ended—with an invitation to follow Him. Peter would, for the rest of his days.

REFLECT

Guilt can be crushingly heavy. It can hinder our relationships with others and our relationship with God. The truth is, there are good reasons to feel guilty. We all fail each other and our Savior in countless ways. Do you wrestle with guilt? Are there memories you wish you did not have, the content of which you fear disqualifies you from truly and fully serving our Lord? What do you need to confess to be able to embrace God's forgiveness and restoration?

God of Restoration, thank You for the example of Peter. His story offers us hope that we are not beyond redemption, that none of our sins keep us from serving You fully and freely. We may not deny knowing You when we are asked, but we perhaps deny You by our actions.

Forgive me for a lack of courage. Restore me when I repent. Help me to confront the memories of my guilt when they try to keep me from doing what You ask or being who You have called me to be. Thank You for offering me restoration freely and frequently. Grant me the strength to face my past and to step into my future. Amen.

40

THE WITNESSES

Matthew 28:16–20; Acts 1:6–9

Then the eleven disciples went to Galilee, to the mountain where Jesus had told them to go. When they saw him, they worshiped him; but some doubted. Then Jesus came to them and said, "All authority in heaven and on earth has been given to me. Therefore go and make disciples of all nations, baptizing them in the name of the Father and of the Son and of the Holy Spirit, and teaching them to obey everything I have commanded you. And surely I am with you always, to the very end of the age." . . .

Then they gathered around him and asked him, "Lord, are you at this time going to restore the kingdom to Israel?"

He said to them: "It is not for you to know

the times or dates the Father has set by his own authority. But you will receive power when the Holy Spirit comes on you; and you will be my witnesses in Jerusalem, and in all Judea and Samaria, and to the ends of the earth."

After he said this, he was taken up before their very eyes, and a cloud hid him from their sight.

In the morning light, a timid group gathered with Jesus on a hillside, shifting from foot to foot in anticipation. The anticipation had been building for years and just a short while earlier, had seemed pointless, but was now higher than ever.

Jesus had just declared that authority—all authority in both heaven and earth—had been given to Him. That authority wasn't really surprising. The disciples had seen Jesus wield it in dozens of ways over the last three years.

They had seen and heard Jesus talk to the demons possessing a man who lived alone in the graves. They had heard the voice of a legion of dark spirits plead with Him for mercy, to allow them to possess something else. Jesus sent them into the pigs, which immediately went crazy and plunged into the sea. Pigs don't swim.

Jesus had shown He could bend the natural world to His command. Caught in a storm, their boat filling with water from above and below, the disciples were afraid they would drown. But it turned out that drowning wasn't the scariest thing in that boat. Jesus was. He stood in the bow and spoke to the storm. Calm replaced the chaos on the sea, and for the disciples, fear of the man in the bow replaced fear of dying in the depths.

And how many people had Jesus healed? Some He had touched. Others He spoke over. Some He healed in person and others from across the province. And once a woman helped herself to a healing from Him. In the middle of a crowd, she forced her way next to Him and grabbed the hem of His robe. She, in her faith, had drawn power from Him, and He knew it. He found her in the crowd and commended her for her faith.

Twice Jesus took what would barely feed a boy and turned it into a feast with enough leftovers to feed another crowd. And the disciples still talked about the wine He created at Cana.

Even death bowed to Jesus's authority. A widow's son, a little girl, Lazarus, and even Jesus

Himself. Jesus snatched all of them free from death's grip.

He really did have authority. The group gathered on the hillside believed it; He had proved it. But never did He turn His authority and power against Rome. Not once did He move to oust Herod or Pilate, let alone Caesar.

The group listened with butterflies in their stomachs as Jesus reminded them that *all* authority was His. Surely, the past years had been building to that moment. The miracles had been a slow burn—building the Messiah's reputation. After the crash of the crucifixion, the elation of the resurrection had evolved into confident expectation—if death couldn't stop Jesus, what chance did Caesar have? Surely the Father's kingdom had come.

Peter remembered this authority Jesus mentioned. He couldn't forget it. So, sometime later, when they were all together again on the Mount of Olives, he pressed the issue. Peter asked Jesus plainly, "Will You now restore the kingdom to Israel?"

It was the question on everyone's lips. How many Jews before them had asked the same question and never heard an answer? Soon they would have the kingdom, the king, the peace and rest. And it all hung in the air around Jesus where He stood, back from the dead, on a hillside that morning. His life, His mission, they thought, is about to be fulfilled.

The expectation grew thick; it shouldered its way into the group and made its presence known as they waited for His answer. Their faces betrayed their eagerness. And then Jesus spoke.

"It is not for you to know the times or dates the Father has set by his own authority."

The wind left their sails as suddenly as it had that night on the Sea of Galilee three years ago. But Jesus wasn't finished.

"But you will receive power when the Holy Spirit comes on you; and you will be my witnesses in Jerusalem, and in all Judea and Samaria, and to the ends of the earth."

Witnesses. That's their job now. To tell people that Jesus has the authority. To tell them who He is and what He has done. To continue what He Himself had been doing. His mission was now their mission. Jesus came to invite people into God's kingdom—not overthrow Rome's. He spent His time demonstrating the life and love of the kingdom. His teaching and His miracles were all directed toward the same end.

And now it was their turn. It was their time to go, in the power of the Holy Spirit, and tell people about Jesus, inviting them into His kingdom.

REFLECT

Perhaps the true test for a disciple of Jesus is whether or not they are a witness, not in the sense of having seen Jesus's earthly ministry firsthand, but in the sense of passing on what they know of Jesus and inviting others into His kingdom. What can you witness to about Jesus? What has He done that you can tell others about as you travel through your own Jerusalem, Judea, and Samaria? What are some reasons you may not witness to what He has done?

Jesus, we have been invited into Your kingdom. It is the kingdom where You have all the power and authority, and where You have given Your people the same mission You had. We are to go out into the world and invite people into

Your kingdom. That was literally the last command You gave Your disciples—to go out into the world and be a witness for You. There are times when we love to talk about all You have done; other times, we shrink back from the opportunity.

I know I am more comfortable talking about You to those who are already part of Your kingdom, those with whom I share a commitment to You. The reason I do not always witness for You is that [fill in your honest reason]. I know You have been given all authority, and in that authority You have told me to witness to who You are and what You have done. Your mission is now mine. Help me to operate in the power and authority of You, my King. Amen.

Help us get the word out!

Our Daily Bread Publishing exists to feed the soul with the Word of God.

If you appreciated this book, please let others know.

- Pick up another copy to give as a gift.
- Share a link to the book or mention it on social media.
- Write a review on your blog, on a book-seller's website, or at our own site (odb.org/store).
- Recommend this book for your church, book club, or small group.

Connect with us:

🅕 @ourdailybread

🅞 @ourdailybread

🅣 @ourdailybread

Our Daily Bread Publishing
PO Box 3566
Grand Rapids, Michigan 49501 USA

✉ books@odb.org